D1806639

Paper Aeroplanes

PAPER
AEROPLANES

How to make aeroplane models from paper

by **RICHARD SLADE**

FABER AND FABER
LONDON

First published in 1970
by Faber and Faber Limited
24 Russell Square London WC1
Printed in Great Britain by
Latimer Trend & Co. Ltd., Whitstable
All rights reserved

ISBN 0 571 09193 8

© *Richard Slade, 1970*

Contents

7

Illustrations

Photographs

Line Drawings

9

11

1 · Tools and Materials

The design of the aeroplane shows that, like the ship, an object which is of great service to man can also be very beautiful.

This is one of the reasons why people enjoy making models of ships and aeroplanes.

Our models are made from cartridge paper, a strong kind of drawing paper which is easily obtainable. The outlines and patterns given are the actual size of the models. The patterns are traced on tracing paper or on greaseproof paper and are then transferred to the cartridge paper. The outlines of the aeroplane serve as a check and guide as you make the model.

These are small models. If you wish you can make larger ones simply by making the squares larger and copying the outlines and patterns on to these larger squares. Cartridge paper will do for models up to about twice as large as the models here; beyond this use thin card. The bigger the model, the stronger must be the modelling medium.

Tools

Scissors
Pencil
Rubber
Ruler
Compasses
Set Square
Sharp penknife or craft tool

Materials

Cartridge paper
Tracing paper
Glue: use something like Evo-Stik Resin 'W'. Squeeze a little of this as required on to a piece of card and apply it with a matchstick shaved thin at one end.

Cocktail sticks or matchsticks
Pins
For stands: balsa wood and wooden balls, wire.

2 · Paper Darts

The joy of the paper dart is to watch it soar, glide, circle and gracefully come to rest on the ground. But they will not always work like this. Sometimes the air is not still enough; or maybe the shape of the dart is wrong.

Here is a way of amusing yourself which, to say the least, is inexpensive. We can experiment for quite a while with a few sheets of paper.

We can make darts that will be best at gliding, or at travelling far, or at doing aerial acrobatics, and so on. It is largely a matter of experiment: altering the shape of the wings, shortening or lengthening the dart, trying out small weights, like paper clips, to give balance and stability.

Plate 1

This shows what may be called the traditional dart.

A. *The most common kind of dart*

1. Take an oblong piece of paper and fold it down the centre lengthwise. Open it out and fold over the corners a and b to meet at the centre crease.
2. Fold over c and d.
3. Close shape by putting e and f together.
4. Fold back e on to g. Fold back f on other side.
5. The top of the finished dart looks like this.

E2 shows the bottom of the dart.

B. *Aeroplane dart*

This was most probably the first ever kind of paper aeroplane: it was already being made during World War 1. There are different ways of making this. One way is shown here.

1. Take an oblong of paper. Fold over one corner and crease. Cut away strip left and put on one side.
2. Open out folded paper and there should be a square. Fold and crease to give the second diagonal: the thin lines on the diagram represent the creases. Open out and fold in half across the dotted line.
3. As shown by the arrows on 2, the creases in the centre are pushed inwards

15

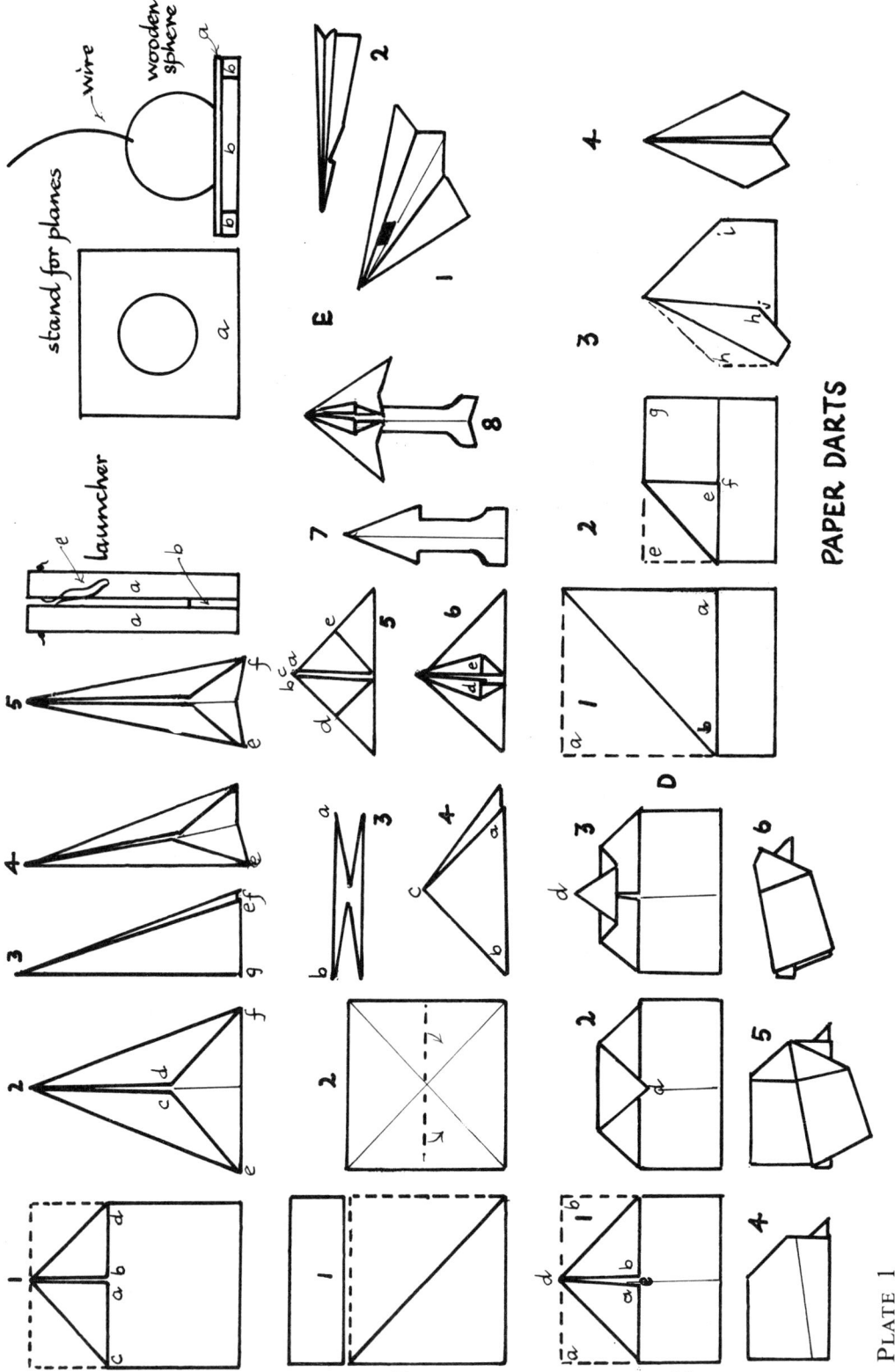

PAPER DARTS

PLATE 1

to give shape 3: viewed from bottom.

4. Same shape seen from front. b corner is free like a.

5. Bend b up to c and a to c.

6. Fold over d and e. This makes the wing shape.

7. Make fuselage and tailplane shape from the strip of paper put on one side.

8. Insert fuselage into wing and shape by bending wings. The nose can be bent underneath, if desired: this will give the dart more carrying power.

C. *Traditional Japanese dart*

1. Take a square of paper. Fold at centre. Open out and fold over a and b to meet at crease.

2. Fold over d.

3. Fold back d.

4. Fold shape in half with parts already folded inside.

5. Fold back part of shape on one side – the thin line on diagram 4 shows where the fold is made.

6. Fold back shape on other side to match.

D. *This is a stronger form of A*

1. Take an oblong of paper. Fold over a to meet opposite edge. Draw line or make crease along ba.

2. Fold over paper to line ba. Bend down corners e and g to meet in centre at f.

3. Bend over h and i to meet in centre at j.

4. Finished shape top view. This has a projecting fin at bottom as at E2.

Launcher

This is made from balsa wood. Two pieces of $\frac{1}{2}''$ square strip, each 12″ long; one piece $3'' \times \frac{1}{2}''$ and $\frac{3}{16}''$ thick. Refer to the diagram on Plate 1. Saw small cuts in the tops of the two pieces aa. Join the pieces aa to the piece b with glue: this can be strengthened by binding it with thin string. Cut a thin rubber band to make a length and knot at each end. Put the rubber length into the saw cuts: e shows the rubber piece.

Plate 2

These are experimental darts.

This is where the fun begins. These are suggested shapes only. You will have to decide on your own size; also small weights, such as paper clips, will most probably have to be attached to these darts, front or centre, to give stability.

1. Single wing. Make cuts in rear edge of wing – shown by lines. Bend back part of each tip. A paper clip will be needed at the nose. Fold on dotted line.

17

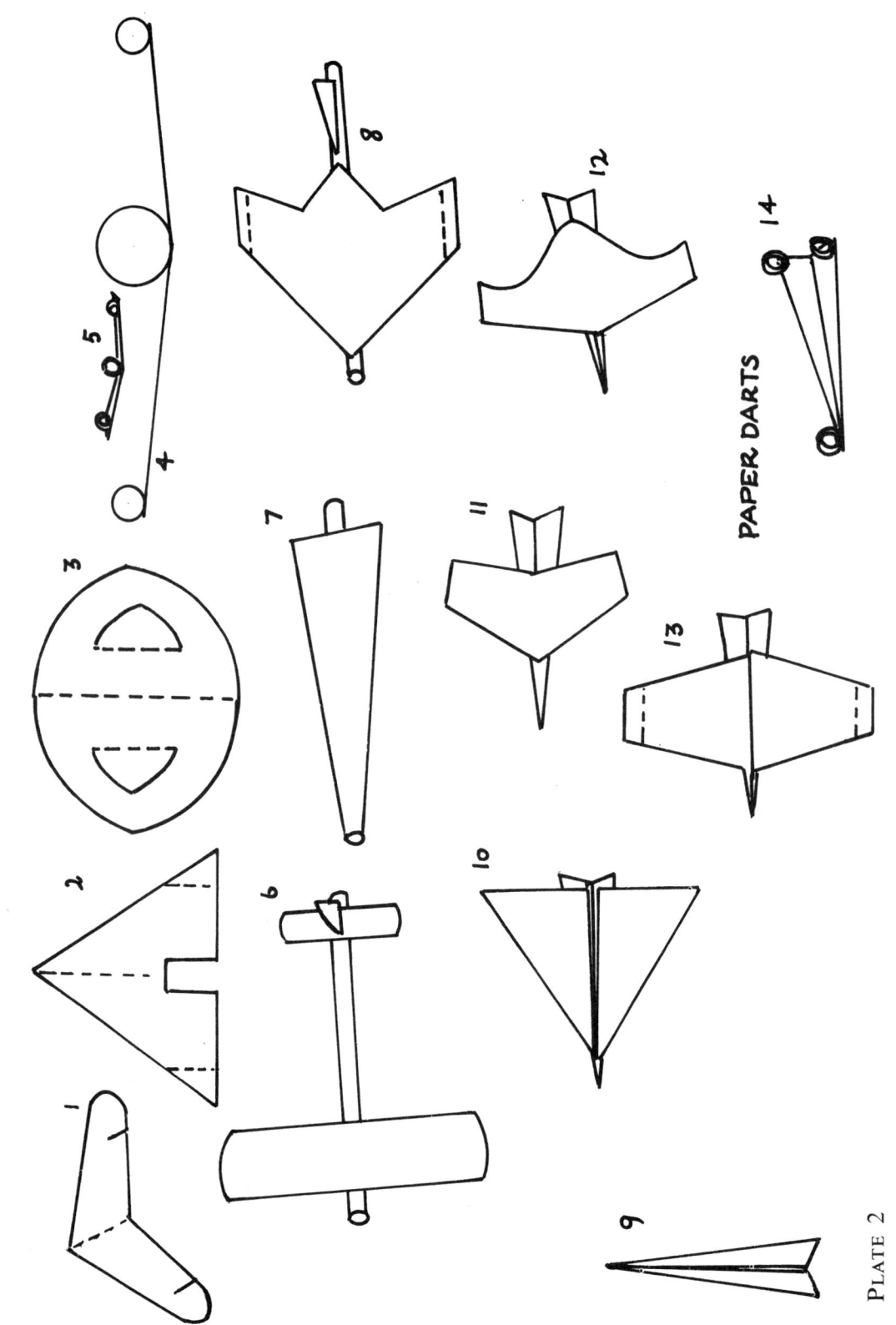

PAPER DARTS

PLATE 2

2. Single wing. Fold inwards on middle dotted line; fold outwards at tips.

3. Cut round lines on inside of shape and fold down cut pieces on dotted lines. Fold up on centre dotted line.

4. Single wing. A strip of paper with narrow tubes of paper glued on top. 5 shows shape.

6, 7 and 8. These all have a thin tube of paper for fuselage. Fins may be added to these.

9, 10, 11, 12, 13 and 14. These use the dart A, Plate 1, as a fuselage–shown at 9. Wings are glued to the top of this. Fins may be added.

3 · Parts of an Aeroplane

A modern aircraft is shown at the top of Plate 3. Its main parts are the fuselage, mainplane or wing, tailplane, fin and engine. The leading edges are those which face the front.

Also shown is a seaplane with its floats. The bottom of the fuselage acts as a float.

An old-type biplane is at the bottom of the plate. This shows the under-carriage and propeller as well as the struts and strengthening wires, which were necessary for this type of aeroplane.

Fuselage

This has to be both strong and light and streamlined. It was formerly made as a covered framework, but now aluminium alloys and laminated plastic can be built up in units to form a tough casing that needs no framework.

Wing

An aeroplane with two wings is called a biplane. An aeroplane with three wings–no longer built–was a triplane. Most aeroplanes of today are mono-planes or single-wing.

When this wing is fixed to the upper part of the fuselage, the aeroplane is known as a high-wing monoplane; in the middle of the fuselage, as a mid-wing monoplane; at the bottom of the fuselage, as a low-wing monoplane.

In addition modern wings have built-in controls. At the rear or trailing edge are ailerons and flaps. The ailerons, at the outer trailing edge, assist in handling the aircraft, and the pilot is able to use them for making turns and correcting the roll of the plane. The flaps, on the inner trailing edge, help to lift and brake the plane.

Tailplane and Fin

These act as stabilisers; that is, they help to keep the plane on an even keel. An aeroplane such as the Delta Dart has a special type of wing which does away with the need for a tailplane. Most planes, however, require one.

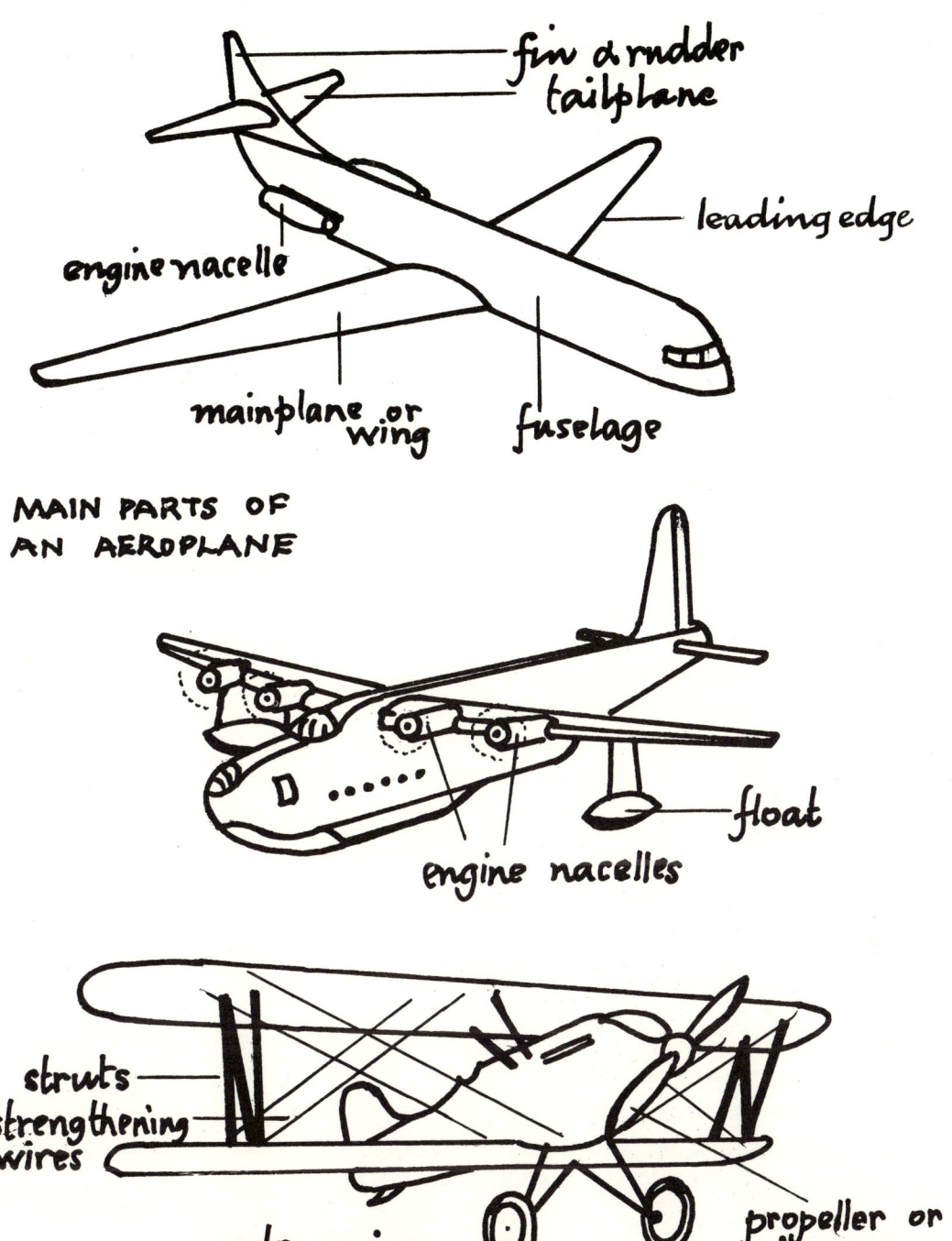

fin a rudder
tailplane

leading edge

engine nacelle

mainplane or
wing

fuselage

MAIN PARTS OF
AN AEROPLANE

float

engine nacelles

struts
strengthening
wires

undercarriage

propeller or
airscrew

PLATE 3

The tailplane acts as a kind of lever that keeps the plane stable along its length. The fin helps to keep the plane upright.

Both tailplane and fin have controls on them. Elevators are fitted to the tailplane, and a rudder to the fin. With these the pilot can make the plane ascend or descend and change direction.

The perfect type of wing has yet to be invented. Some are good for one sort of job, some for another. This is why we see so many different shapes. If you experiment with paper darts, you will realise how the variations in the shape of a wing alter the performance of an aeroplane.

Engine

The engine supplies the power to raise the aircraft from the ground and keep it flying. The petrol, cylinder type engine drives a propeller, which is rather like a ship's screw. Just as the screw takes a 'grip' on the water, so the propeller takes a 'grip' on the air and pulls or thrusts the plane forward.

The petrol engine has heavy, moving parts and this is why aeroplanes with these engines cannot attain very high speeds. The jet engine eliminates these moving parts by making use of the air itself; a small jet can suck in the air to create tremendous power. A gas jet is produced behind the engine to thrust the aircraft forward.

A turbo-prop combines the use of a propeller with a jet engine. Whilst a jet gives much greater speeds when the aircraft is flying high, a propeller is better for the slower speeds required for take-off and landing.

Undercarriage

In earlier aeroplanes the undercarriage was fixed; and there was usually a small wheel, or a skid, at the tail end of the plane.

Most modern undercarriages are retractable, which means that they can be housed in the aircraft when it is flying to improve the streamlining. Small aircraft house their undercarriage in the wing. Large aircraft can draw the undercarriage into the fuselage.

It has been found safer on heavy aircraft to have several small wheels instead of two large ones, and also to provide a third wheelcarriage beneath the nose of the plane to increase the safety and assist in the braking.

4 · Method for Making Cartridge Paper Models

Fuselage

This is the most difficult part in the making of these models. However, it is made as simple as possible by ignoring detail. The general shape is correct. Greater accuracy may be achieved by using the papier mâché method described at the end of the book.

The cartridge paper fuselage begins as an oblong of paper. Draw the pattern on this and cut it out. A tracing of the pattern can be made on tracing paper or greaseproof paper. Put the paper over the pattern and go over it in pencil. Reverse this tracing, put it on the cartridge paper and go over the back of the tracing with pencil. This will transfer the drawing–the first pencil lines –to the paper. The tracing paper can be kept still with paper clips, and a ruler can be used for making the straight lines. This is an easy way of transferring all the patterns to the cartridge paper. If the traced lines appear too faint for cutting out, go over them again in pencil.

Cut out the fuselage pattern and roll it lengthwise round a piece of dowel. A thick, round pencil will do; but if you intend to make several models, then collect a few short lengths of dowel of different diameters, as they will be found very useful in shaping fuselages, engines and floats which need to be curved.

When the paper more or less stays in place as a tube shape, glue where shown. Use a strong glue.

Much of the frustration in modelmaking comes from using a glue or paste which will not stick readily. Even with a strong glue, exercise a little patience and allow it to set before proceeding with the next step.

The next step is to shape the ends of the fuselage by bending the cut parts, sometimes tapered, to meet and gluing them together. When the glue is quite dry, the shape can be further moulded with the fingers, for example, into an oval shape along its length.

Other parts are added to complete the fuselage. Sometimes a nacelle head is put over the front of the fuselage; sometimes small cones are inserted in each end of the fuselage to complete the shape.

When cutting out the cockpit hood pattern, first cut away the inside parts of the pattern with a sharp knife, as this will lessen the risk of tearing the paper. The outside lines can then be cut around with scissors.

Wings

These are made from a double thickness of cartridge paper. This both strengthens and improves the appearance of the model.

Draw the pattern on a single sheet and fold this so that the fold comes on the front or leading edge of the wing. Cut the paper double and leave the fold.

The wing is usually made in two halves for gluing into the fuselage. One should be checked on the other for accuracy.

Slits are made at the right place each side of the fuselage and the wing halves glued in. Glue can also be put on the facing edges of each half wing so that when they meet inside the fuselage they stick together.

When modelling a plane, checks can be made by placing the model over the outline of the aeroplane you are making. If the model is turned upside down the wing and fuselage should fit the outline.

Fin

The fin is made from a double thickness of cartridge paper. The pattern is drawn on a single sheet, which is then folded to give a double thickness before cutting out.

Cut a slit in the back of the fuselage to take the fin. The fin is usually glued in before the tailplane is put on.

Make sure to set it centrally, checking this against the wing and the fuselage.

Tailplane

This is made from a double thickness of cartridge paper and may be made as a whole or in two halves. It will usually be found necessary to cut it in half for assembly.

Draw the pattern on a single sheet and double this so that the fold comes on the leading edge.

Where applicable cut slits on each side of the fuselage by the fin and glue in the tailplane. On some models the tailplane is glued to the fin.

Struts and Undercarriage

Only main struts are given. Where struts exist, especially in older planes, there were usually a number of stay wires also. These are not shown on the models, but a reference to books listed under 'Books about Aircraft' should be made if you are interested.

The struts are glued on when convenient. Any wings to be attached to the fuselage should be in place before the struts.

In the case of the biplanes the struts are first glued on the bottom wing and the top wing is glued on to these.

Wheels should be of double thickness.

5 · Paper Aeroplanes

Sopwith Camel: U.K. 1917

PHOTOGRAPH 1

Single-seat fighter of World War I; span 28 ft.; length 18ft. 9 in.; maximum speed 110 m.p.h.

Patterns

Trace and cut fuselage pattern. Shape round a piece of dowel or pencil to make a tube and glue where shaded (remove cockpit hole before gluing). Let this dry, then glue a, b and c to form shape of end of fuselage.

Make wings and tailplane and fin from double thickness of cartridge paper. Cut slits in back of fuselage to take fin and tailplane. Glue in fin. Cut tailplane

26

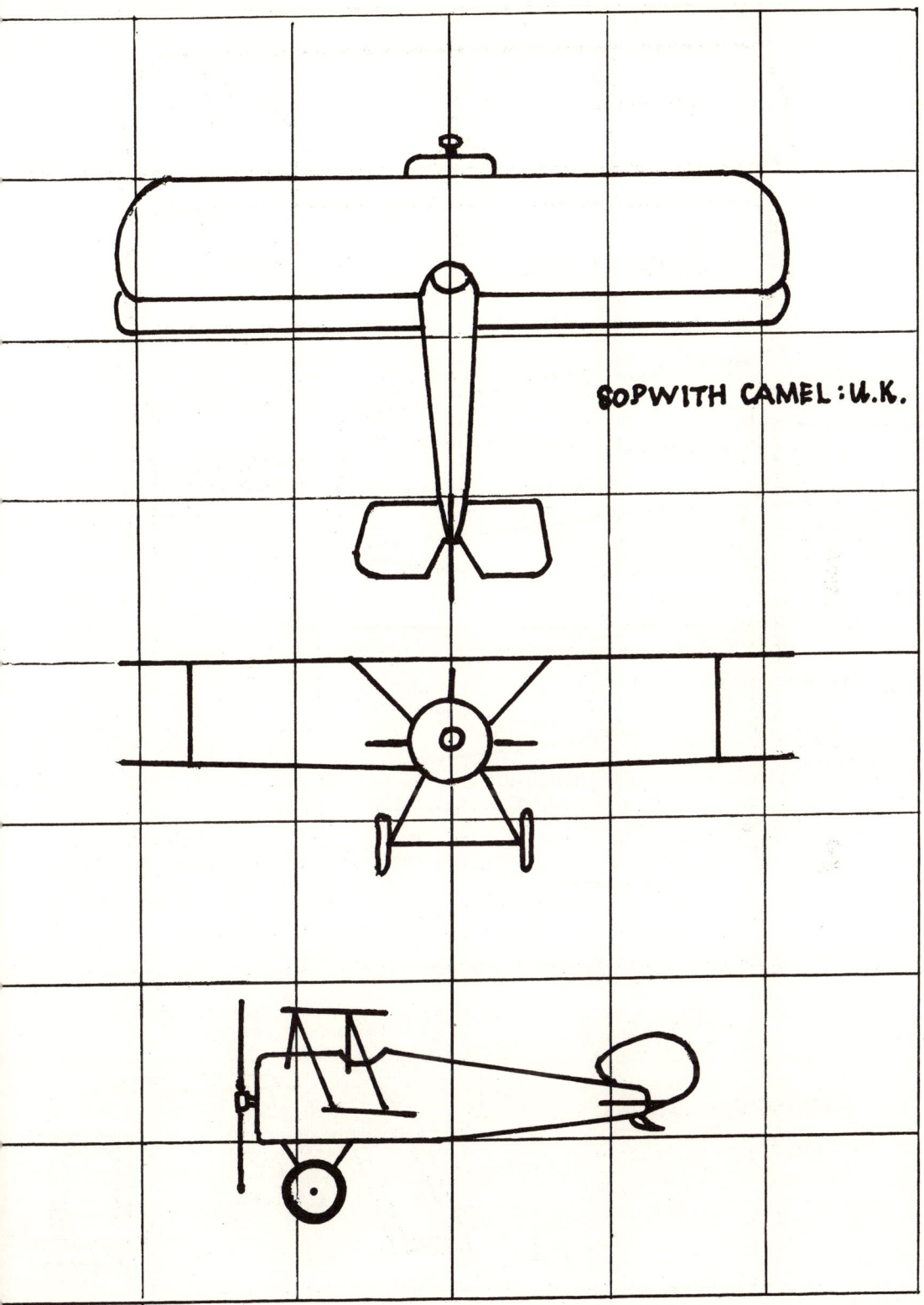

SOPWITH CAMEL: U.K.

PLATE 4

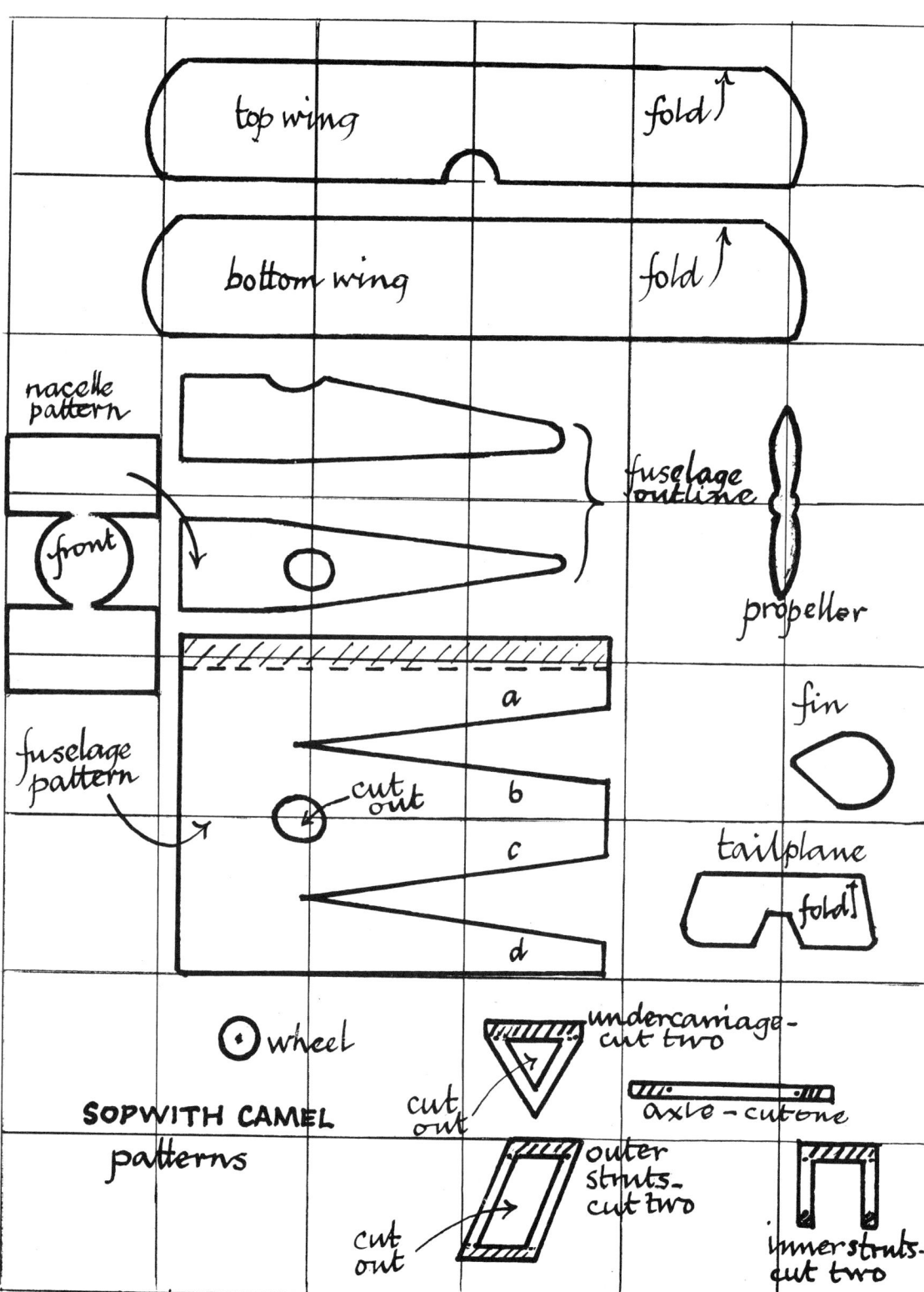

top wing   fold

bottom wing   fold

nacelle pattern

front

fuselage outline

propeller

fin

fuselage pattern

a

b

c

d

cut out

tailplane   fold

wheel

undercarriage – cut two

cut out

axle – cut one

SOPWITH CAMEL
patterns

cut out

outer struts – cut two

inner struts – cut two

PLATE 5

in half and glue one half in each side of fuselage.

Cut bottom wing in half and make slits in fuselage to take bottom wing. Glue in wing, half each side: these should meet in the centre of the fuselage, and the edges that meet can be given a dab of glue.

Cut out main struts and glue to bottom wing. Glue top wing to struts: check for correct position, Plate 4.

Make nacelle. The oblong shapes at each side of pattern are curved round and glued together to fit over front of fuselage.

Cut and fit undercarriage and wheels.

Make propeller. Make a tiny tube of paper and place this over pin to go between propeller and fuselage. The propeller is pinned to the centre of the nacelle.

Fokker DV11: Germany 1918

PHOTOGRAPH 2

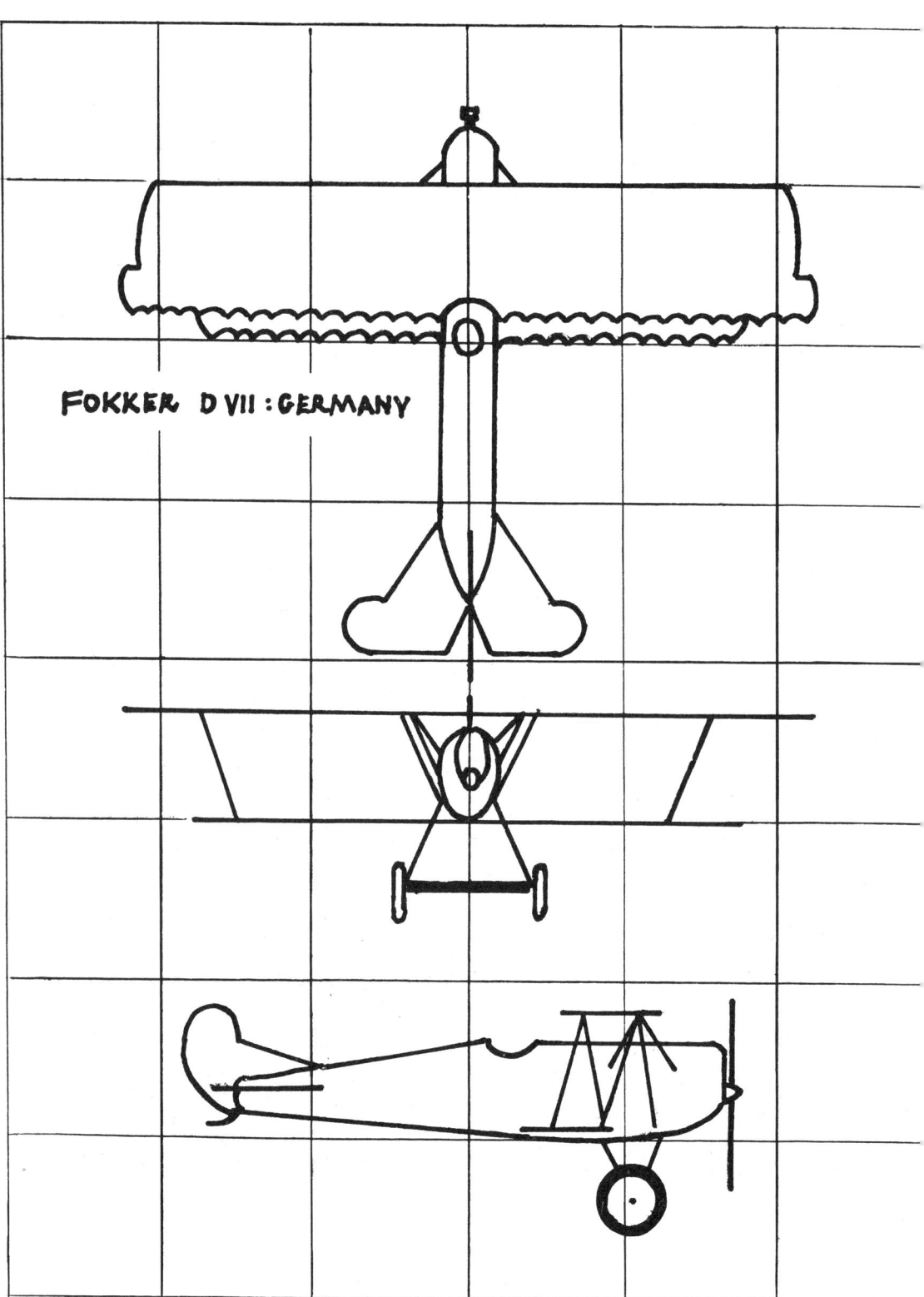

FOKKER D VII : GERMANY

PLATE 6

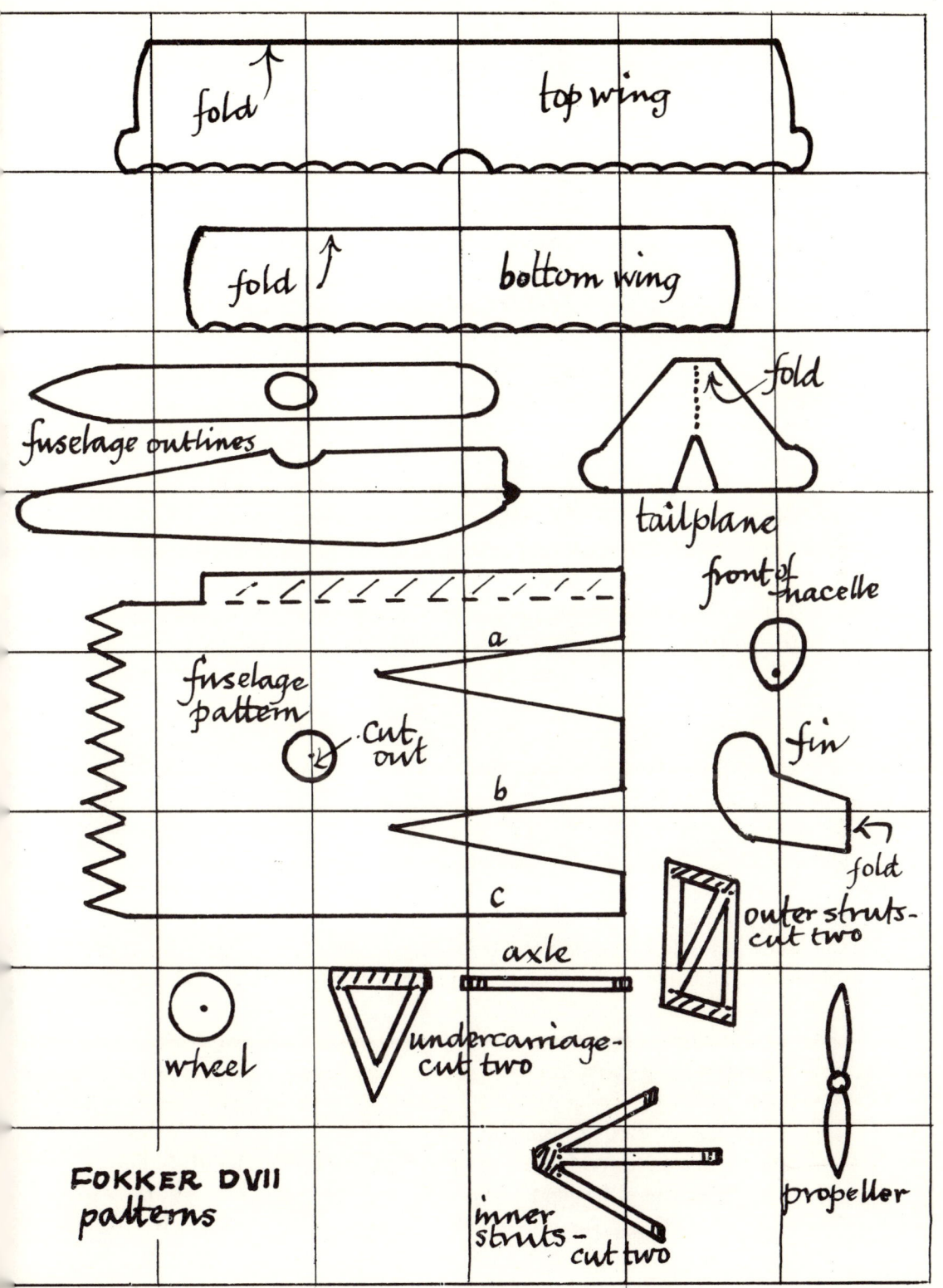

fold ↑   top wing

fold ↑   bottom wing

fuselage outlines

fold

tailplane

front of nacelle

fuselage pattern

a

cut out

b

fin

c

fold

outer struts-
cut two

axle

wheel

undercarriage-
cut two

inner
struts-
cut two

propeller

FOKKER DVII
patterns

PLATE 7

Single-seat fighter of World War I. An easy plane to fly and handle, it was later used by the Dutch as a trainer plane. Span 29 ft. 2 in.; length 22 ft. 10 in.; maximum speed 116 m.p.h.

Patterns

Cut out wings, tailplane and fin in double thickness. Trace patterns for these on a single sheet of cartridge paper and fold before cutting out, so that the fold comes where shown on the pattern.

Trace and cut out fuselage pattern. Shape into a tube and glue in position at shaded portion. The pointed tabs at the nose are bent down and the front of nacelle piece glued over them. a, b and c are shaped to a point and glued together to form rear of fuselage.

Make slits in rear of fuselage and glue in tailplane and fin. Tailplane goes in first: make a cut in this where shown by dotted line to take fin.

Cut bottom wing in half and glue in one half each side of fuselage: make small slits in fuselage for this. When this wing is fast glue on outer struts, taking care to position them correctly by reference to Plate 6. Glue top wing to outer struts. Glue inner struts to fuselage and top wing.

Cut out and fix undercarriage and wheels. Make wheels of double thickness.

Make propeller and pin in place with a tiny tube of paper in front.

Standard E1: U.S.A. 1918

Single-seat fighter-trainer. Span 24 ft.; length 18 ft. 10 in.; maximum speed 100 m.p.h. Not unlike the Sopwith planes, but too slow for combat.

Patterns

Cut wings from double thickness: trace on a single sheet of cartridge paper, fold where indicated so that fold becomes leading edge of wing. Do the same with tailplane and fin.

Trace and cut out fuselage pattern. Before shaping remove cockpit hole from pattern with a sharp knife. Shape fuselage, using a piece of dowel or something similar on which to roll the shape. Glue shaded portion to form tube. Shape rear of fuselage and glue.

Cut out nacelle pattern. Mark centre of circle for propeller. Bend oblongs on pattern and glue round fuselage.

PHOTOGRAPH 3

Cut out and glue cockpit head immediately behind cockpit hole: the line behind the cockpit hole in the pattern shows a cut, and this is opened out slightly to make the cockpit head slope backwards.

Cut bottom wing in half; make small slits each side in bottom of fuselage and glue in each half.

Cut out and attach outer struts to bottom wing: see that these struts slope in the right direction. Attach top wing to outer struts. Check with Plate 8 for position. Attach inner struts to fuselage and top wing.

Cut out and fix undercarriage and wheels.

Make propeller and fix in place with pin. Glue a tiny cone of paper over the head of pin.

33

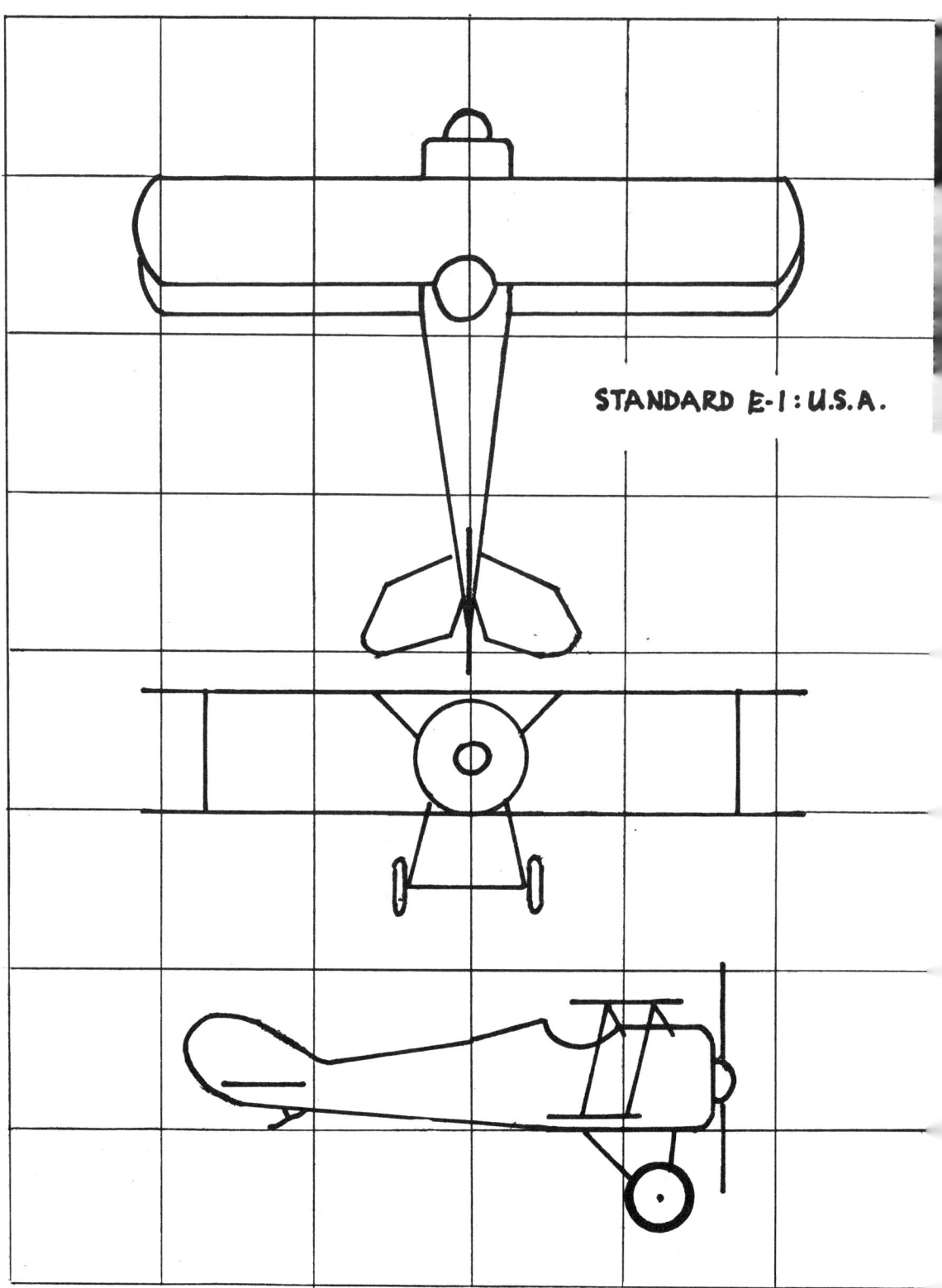

STANDARD E-1 : U.S.A.

PLATE 8

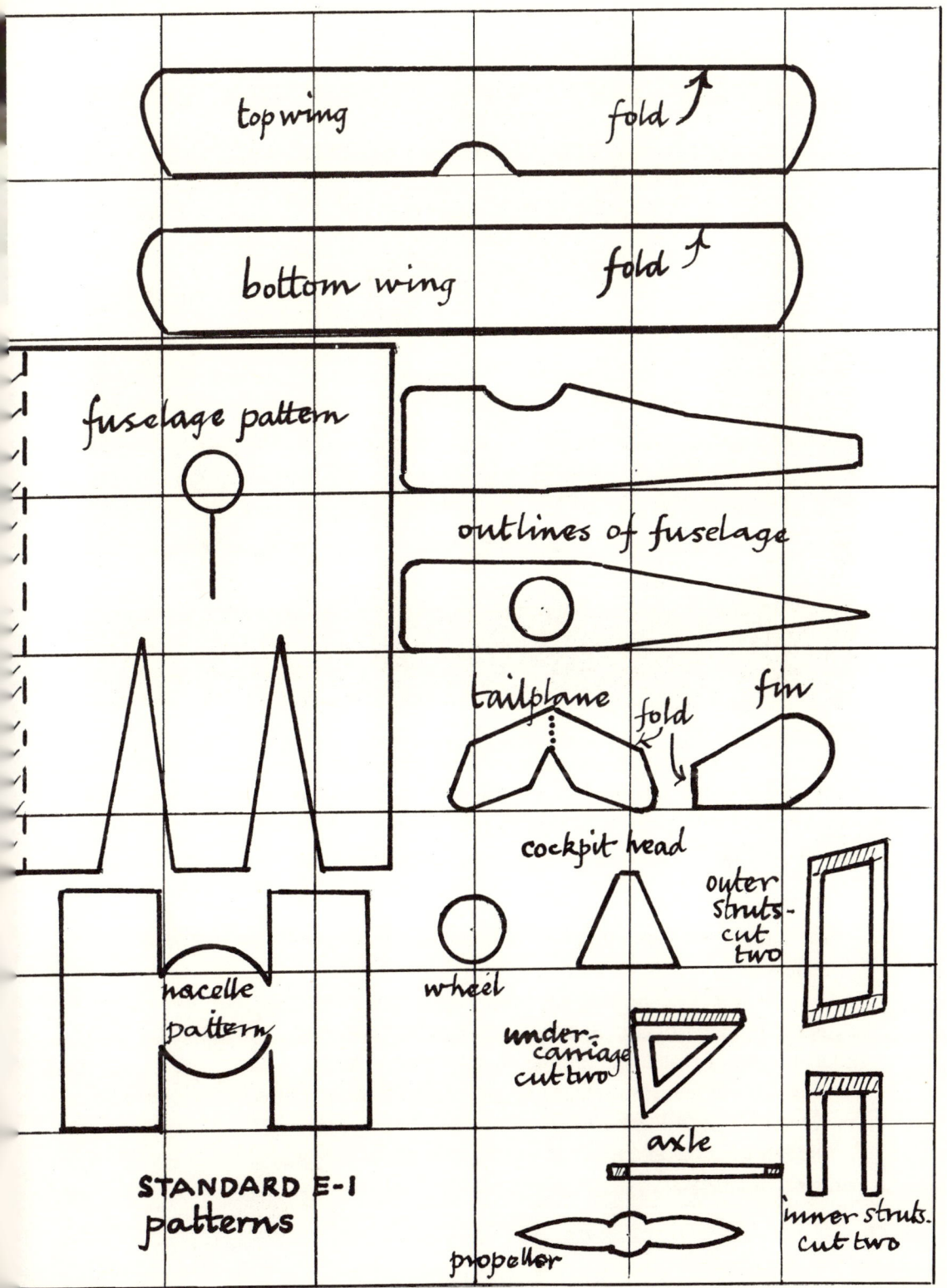

top wing   fold ↗

bottom wing   fold ↗

fuselage pattern

outlines of fuselage

tailplane   fold   fin

cockpit head

nacelle pattern

wheel

outer struts- cut two

under-carriage cut two

axle

inner struts. cut two

propeller

STANDARD E-1 patterns

PLATE 9

Macchi-Castoldi MC 72: Italy 1933

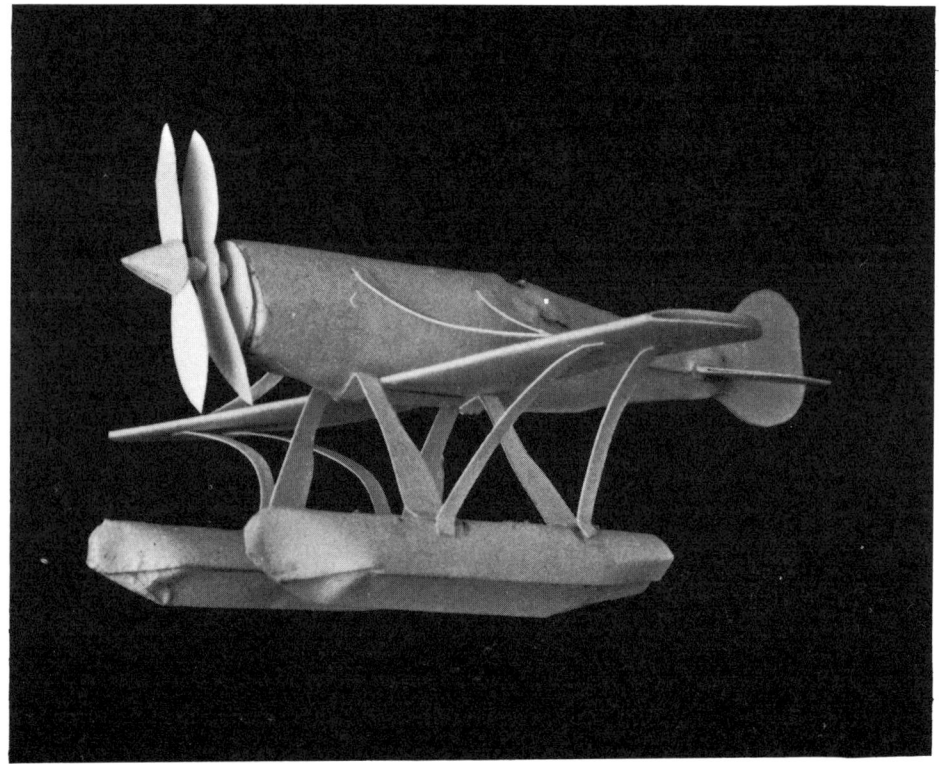

PHOTOGRAPH 4

Seaplane. Winner of Schneider Trophy Contest (a racing contest for seaplanes only) in 1934 with a speed of 440.5 m.p.h., a record for piston engine seaplanes which is still unbroken. Span 31 ft. 1 in.; length 27 ft. 3 in.

Patterns

Trace and cut out wing, tailplane and fin: fold where indicated to give double thickness.

Cut out fuselage pattern; cut out cockpit hole. Shape pattern into a tube, gluing at shaded portion. Shape rear of fuselage and glue. Bend down pointed tabs at front of fuselage and glue nacelle head to these.

Make slits in rear of fuselage and glue in tailplane and fin. Correct positions are obtained from Plate 10.

Glue in wing. Make a slit at the bottom of the fuselage for this and push wing through.

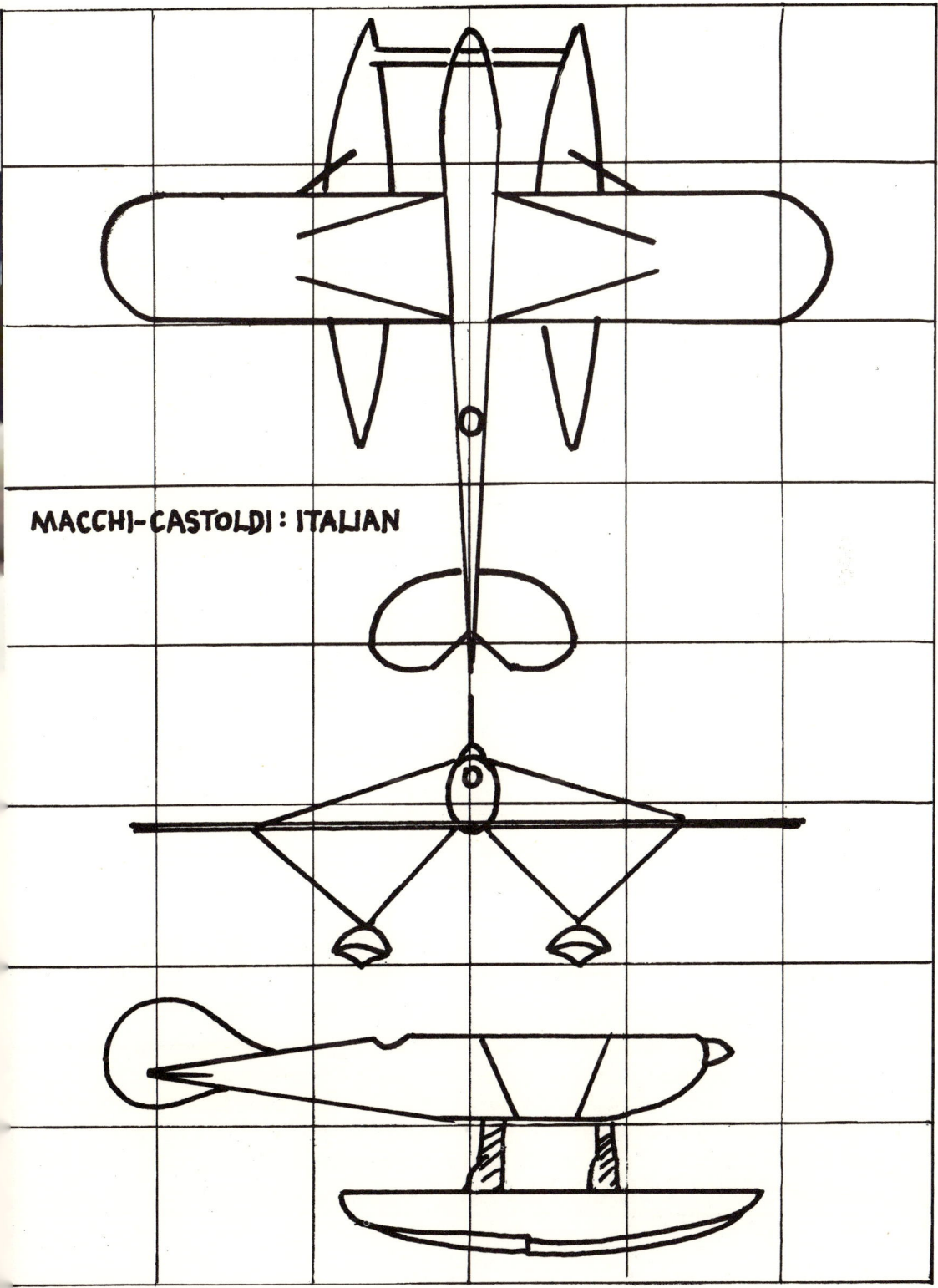

MACCHI-CASTOLDI: ITALIAN

PLATE 10

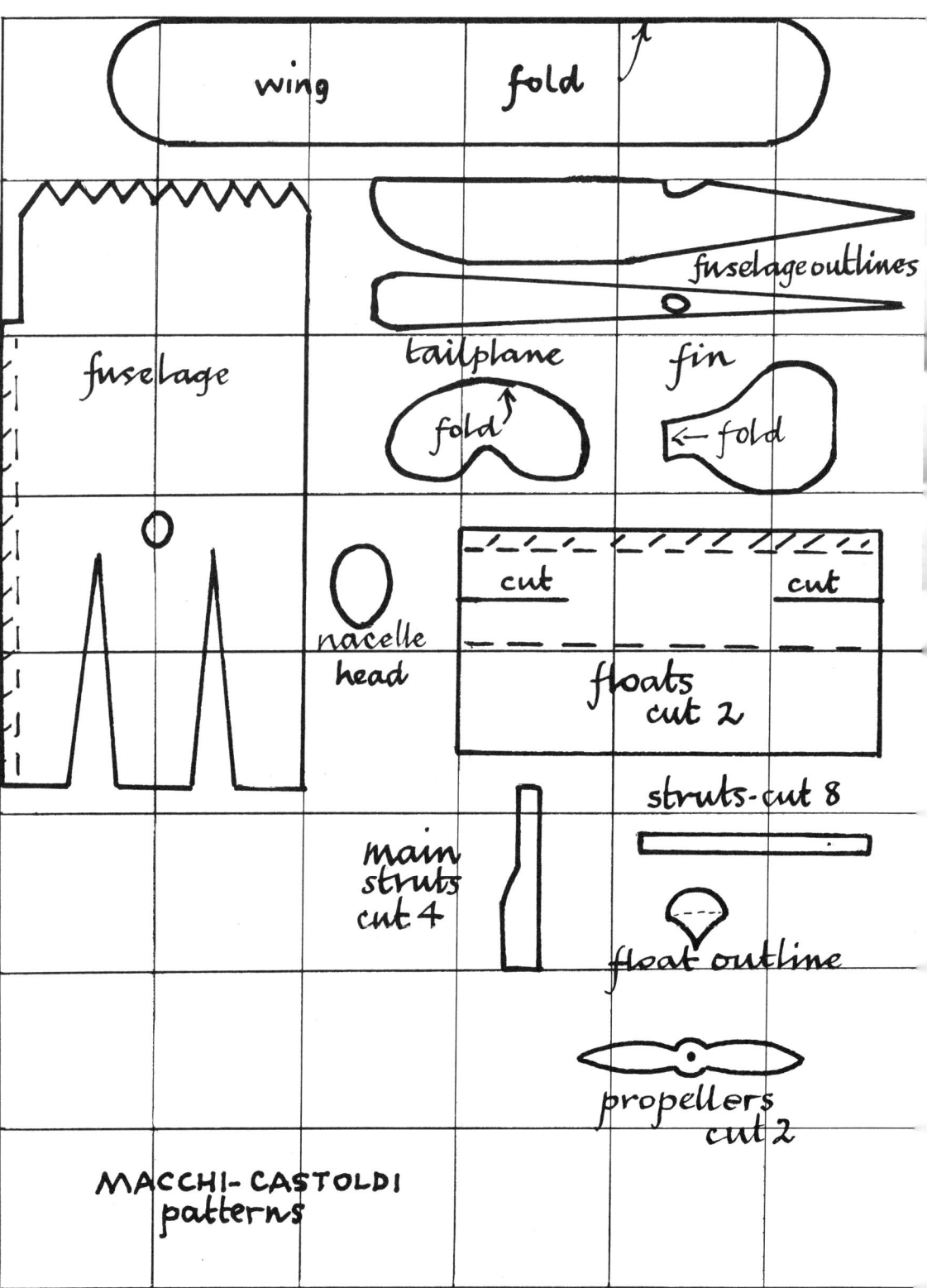

wing   fold

fuselage outlines

fuselage   tailplane   fin

fold   ← fold

nacelle head

cut   cut

floats cut 2

struts · cut 8

main struts cut 4

float outline

propellers cut 2

MACCHI - CASTOLDI patterns

PLATE 11

Attach two struts at each side on top of wing to fuselage.

Make two floats by forming tubes from the pattern; a cut at each end will help to shape the float.

Attach each float to fuselage with the two, main, inner struts. Attach to wing with two outer struts.

Cut two propellers. Attach to nacelle head with pin, separating the propellers with a tiny paper tube; cover head of pin with a tiny cone.

Gloster Gladiator: U.K. 1937

PHOTOGRAPH 5

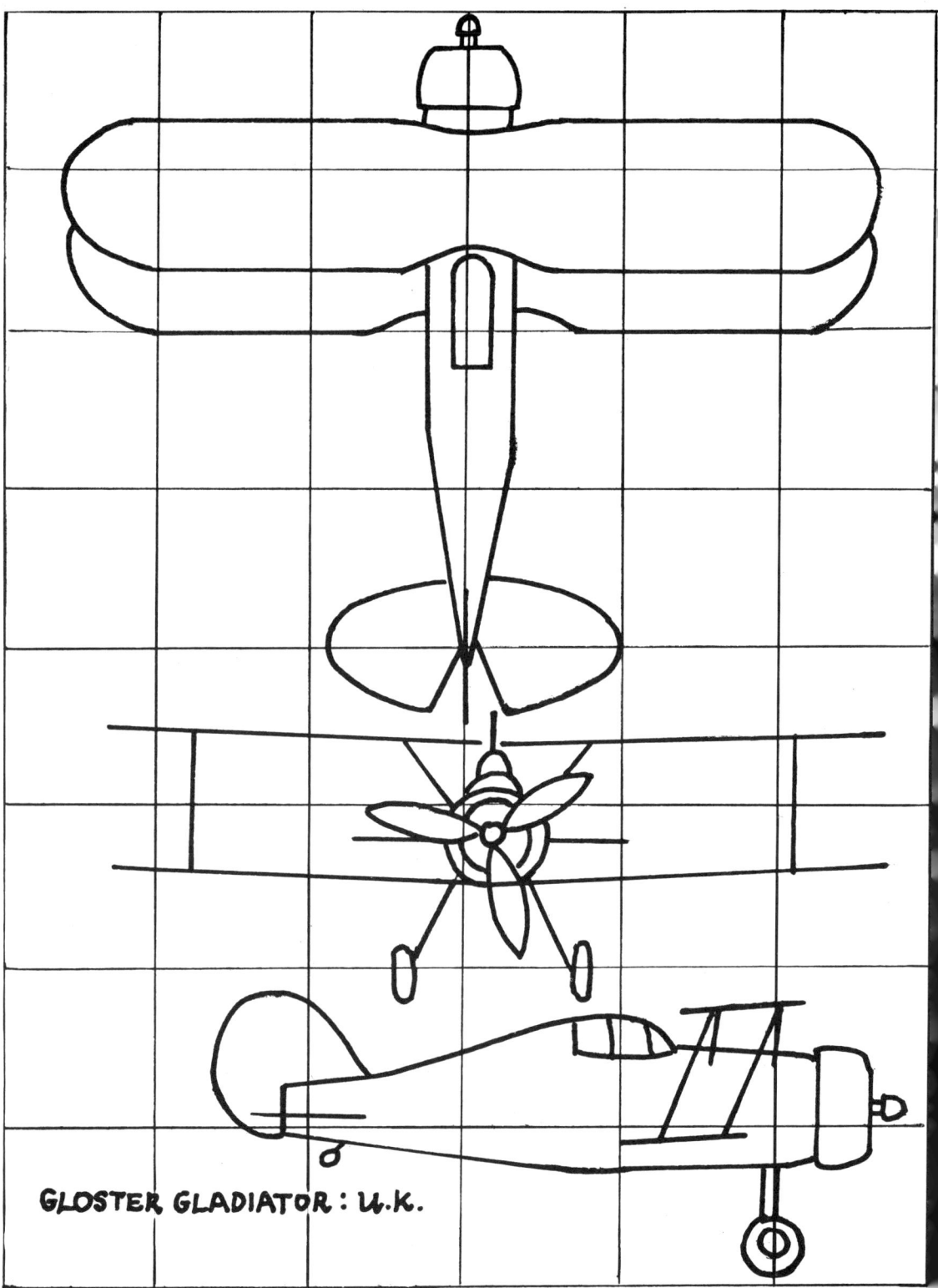

GLOSTER GLADIATOR : U.K.

PLATE 12

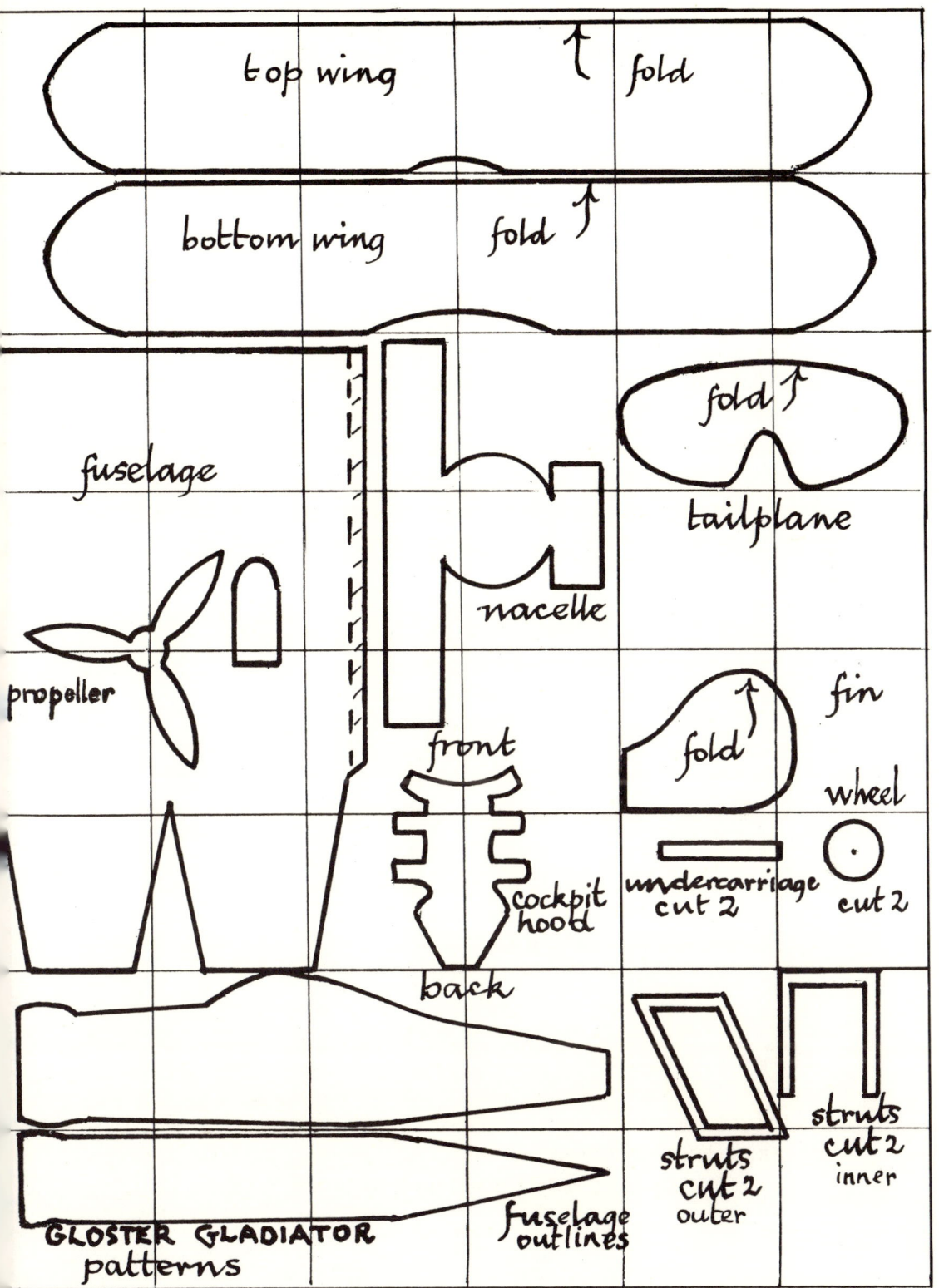

top wing   fold

bottom wing   fold

fuselage   tailplane

nacelle

fold

propeller   fin

front   wheel

undercarriage   cut 2
cut 2

cockpit
hood

back   struts
cut 2   struts
outer   cut 2
inner

GLOSTER GLADIATOR   fuselage
patterns   outlines

PLATE 13

Single-seat fighter. Britain's last biplane fighter. Three famous Gladiators called Faith, Hope and Charity were on service in Malta during World War 2: Faith can be seen in a museum there. Span 32 ft. 3 in.; length 27 ft. 5 in.; maximum speed 253 m.p.h.

Patterns

Trace and cut out wings, tailplane and fin. Trace on single sheet of paper, fold where indicated and cut double thickness.

Trace and cut out fuselage – ignore propeller pattern. Cut out cockpit hole with a sharp knife. Shape fuselage pattern round a piece of dowel and glue at shaded portion.

Make cockpit hood and glue over cockpit.

Cut slits at rear of fuselage and glue in tailplane and fin.

Glue in bottom wing: make slits each side of fuselage at bottom, cut wing in half and glue each half into fuselage. Check position of parts on Plate 12.

Attach outer struts to bottom wing. Attach top wing to outer struts: note that position of top wing is forward of bottom wing. Glue inner struts to fuselage and top wing.

Make nacelle and fit over front of fuselage.

Make undercarriage, with wheels of double thickness.

Make propeller: fix with pin with tiny tube of paper between propeller and nacelle and a tiny cone over the head of pin.

Messerschmitt 109: Germany 1935

A version of this fighter aircraft was the most widely used German fighter of World War 2: more than 33,000 were built. Span 32 ft. $6\frac{1}{2}$ in.; length 29 ft. $0\frac{1}{2}$ in.; maximum speed 354 m.p.h.

Patterns

Trace and cut out fuselage and remove cockpit hole with a sharp knife. Shape fuselage pattern round a piece of dowel and glue shaded portion to form tube. Shape rear of fuselage and glue. Shape front of fuselage: glue the two long edges together and bend down pointed tabs. Glue fuselage front to tabs. Mark centre of front for propeller.

Trace and cut out wing, tailplane and fin from double thickness.

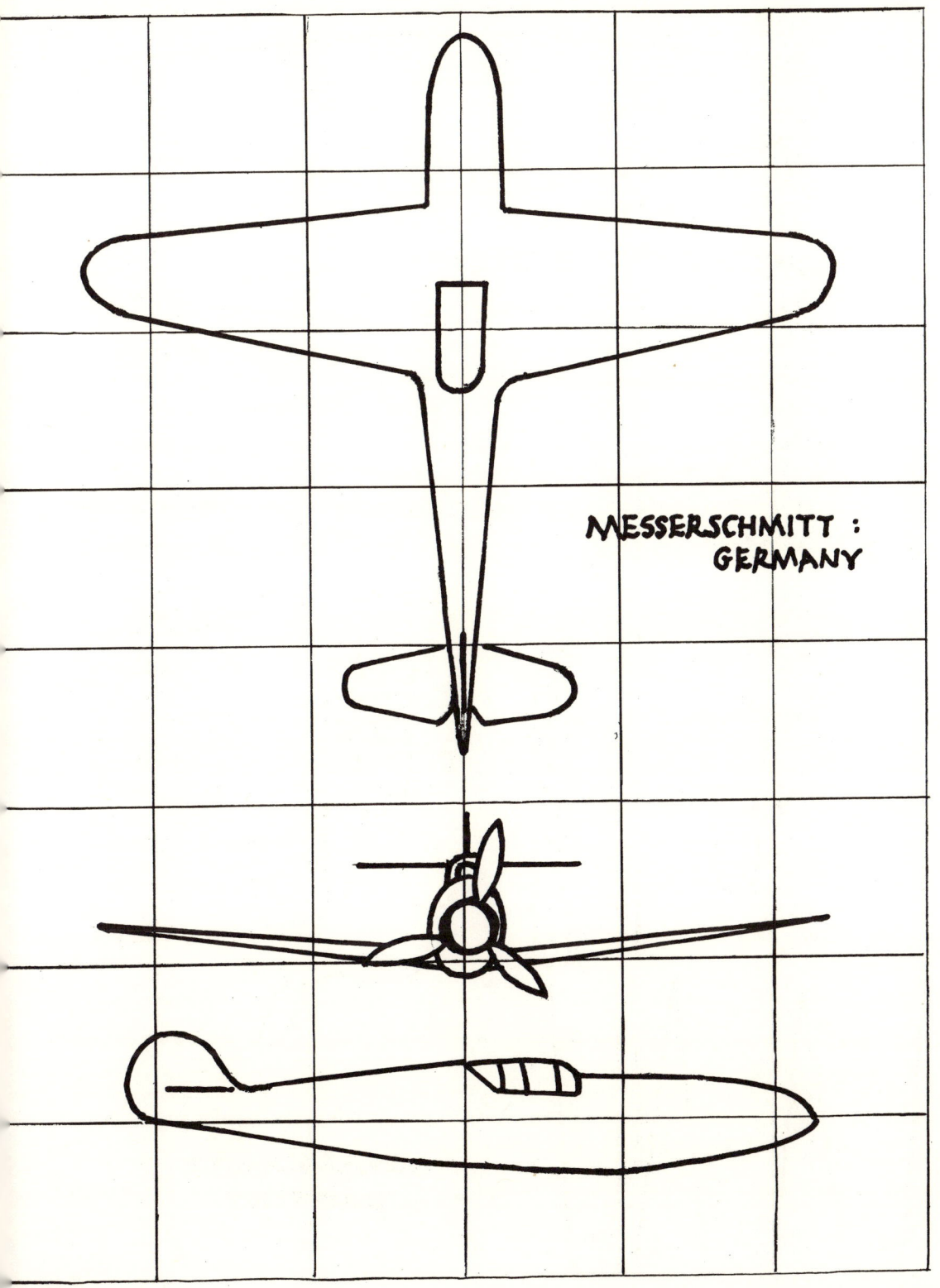

MESSERSCHMITT :
GERMANY

PLATE 14

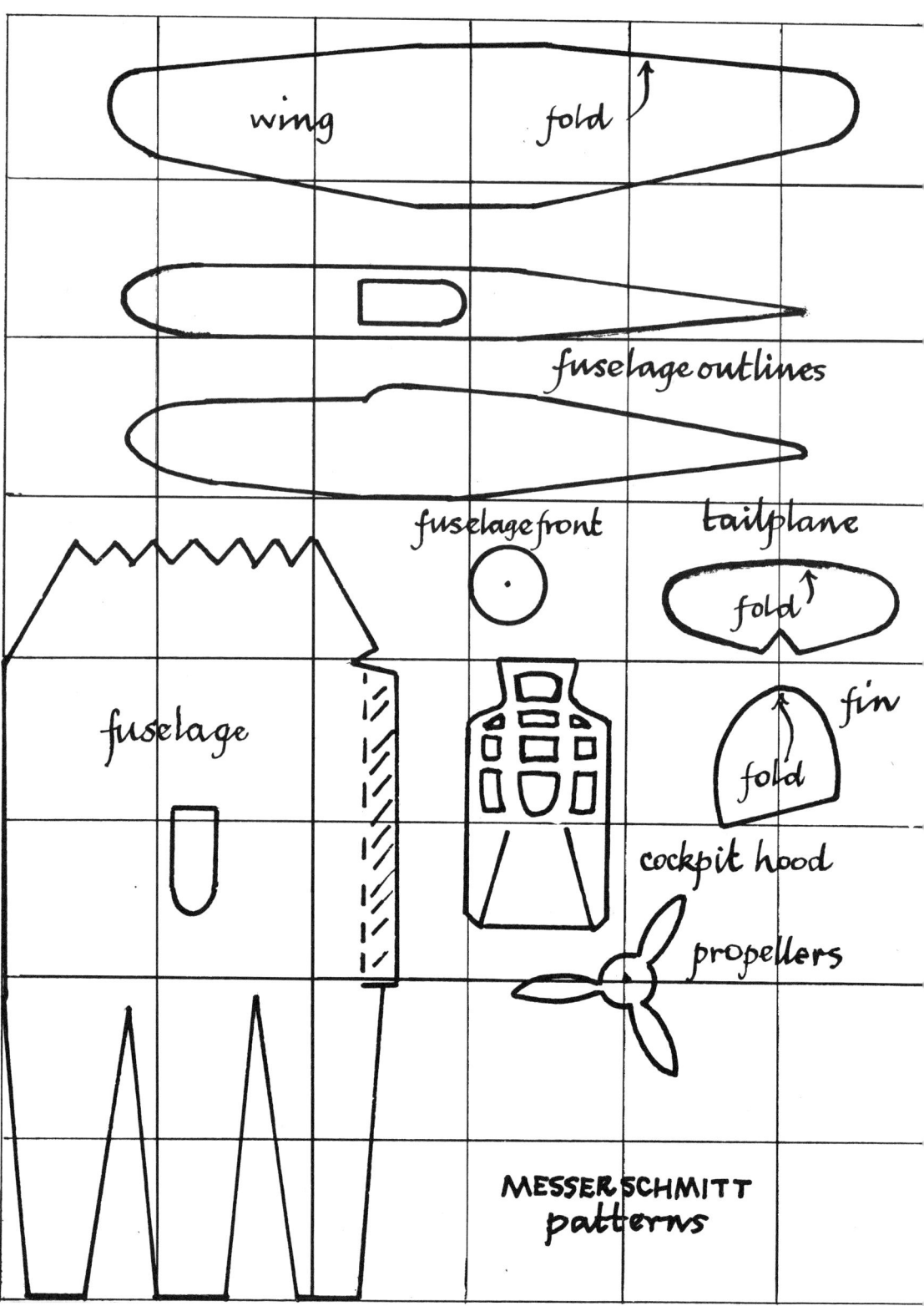

wing

fold

fuselage outlines

fuselage front

tailplane

fold

fin

fuselage

fold

cockpit hood

propellers

MESSERSCHMITT
patterns

PLATE 15

PHOTOGRAPH 6

Make slits in rear of fuselage and glue in fin and tailplane.

Make cockpit hood. Cut along oblique lines inside pattern; shape and glue hood in position. Remember to cut out the windows in the pattern before cutting round the outside, as this will help to prevent tearing.

Attach wing at bottom of fuselage by cutting slit and pushing the wing through this and gluing. Check for position on Plate 14.

Make propeller and small cone. Cut cone in half and glue bottom half to fuselage front. Pin propeller through this to fuselage and cover head of pin with top of cone.

Grumman F3F: U.S.A. 1935

Navy carrier-based single-seat biplane fighter. Span 32 ft.; length 23 ft. $3\frac{1}{2}$ in.; maximum speed 226 m.p.h.

PHOTOGRAPH 7

Patterns

Trace and cut out wings, tailplane and fin on single sheet, fold and cut double thickness.

Trace and cut out fuselage pattern. Remove cockpit hole with sharp knife. Shape fuselage round a piece of dowel and glue at shaded portion to form tube. Shape and glue rear of fuselage. Cut front of fuselage where shown: the nacelle is slightly smaller than the front of the fuselage and the cuts will enable it to go over the front.

Make slits at rear of fuselage and glue in fin and tailplane.

Make cockpit hood: cut out windows before cutting round outline. Shape hood and fit.

46

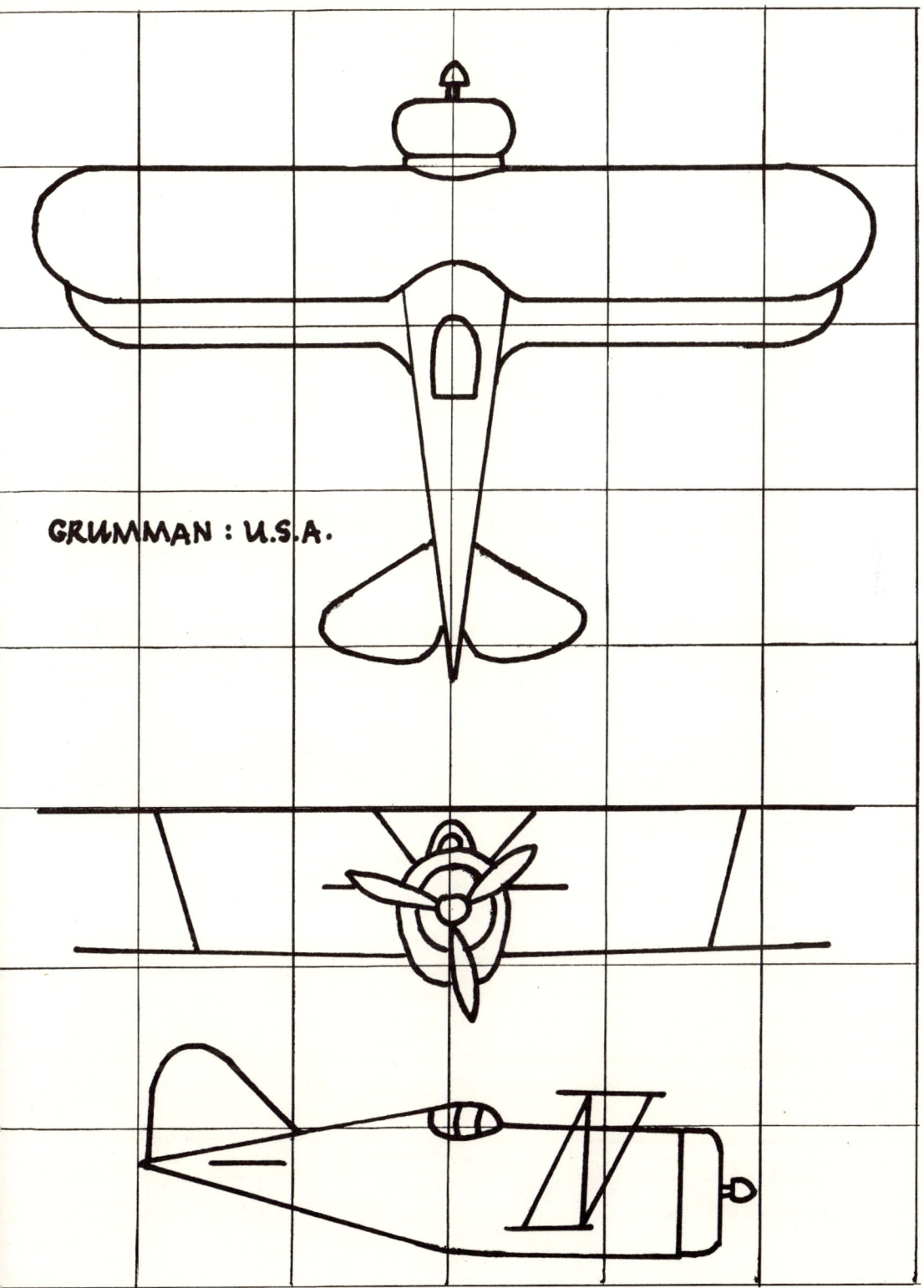

GRUMMAN : U.S.A.

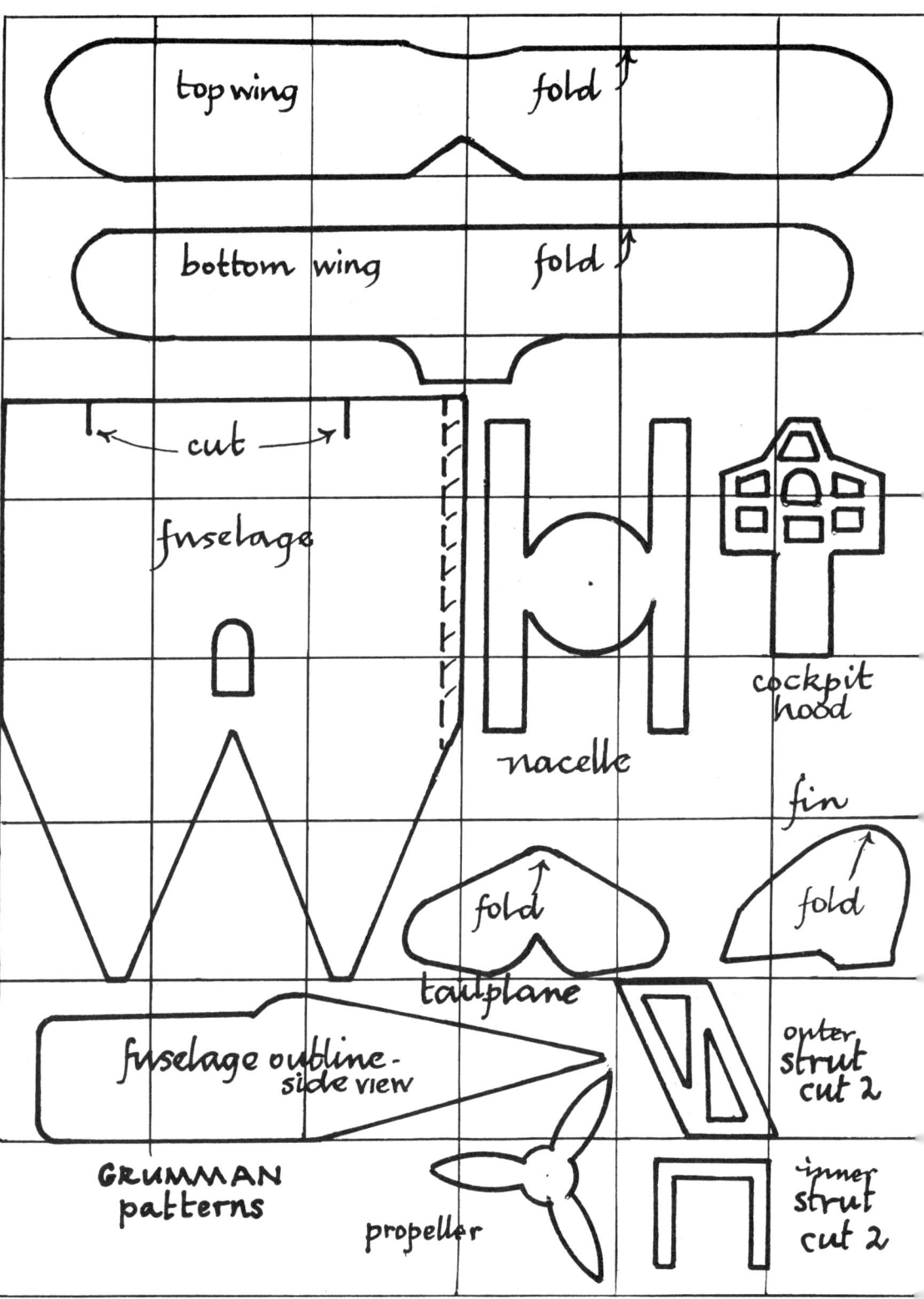

top wing fold

bottom wing fold

cut

fuselage

nacelle

cockpit hood

fin

fold

fold

taılplane

fuselage oulline - side view

GRUMMAN patterns

propeller

outer strut cut 2

inner strut cut 2

PLATE 17

Cut and shape nacelle: the two side strips fit round the outside of the fuselage and should be a little less in diameter. Mark centre of nacelle head for propeller.

Fix bottom wing. First cut wing in half; make slits at bottom of fuselage and glue in wing halves, which should meet inside the fuselage.

Attach outer struts to bottom wing. Glue on top wing to these struts: note the top wing comes forward.

Attach inner struts to fuselage and top wing.

Wellington: U.K. 1939

PHOTOGRAPH 8

49

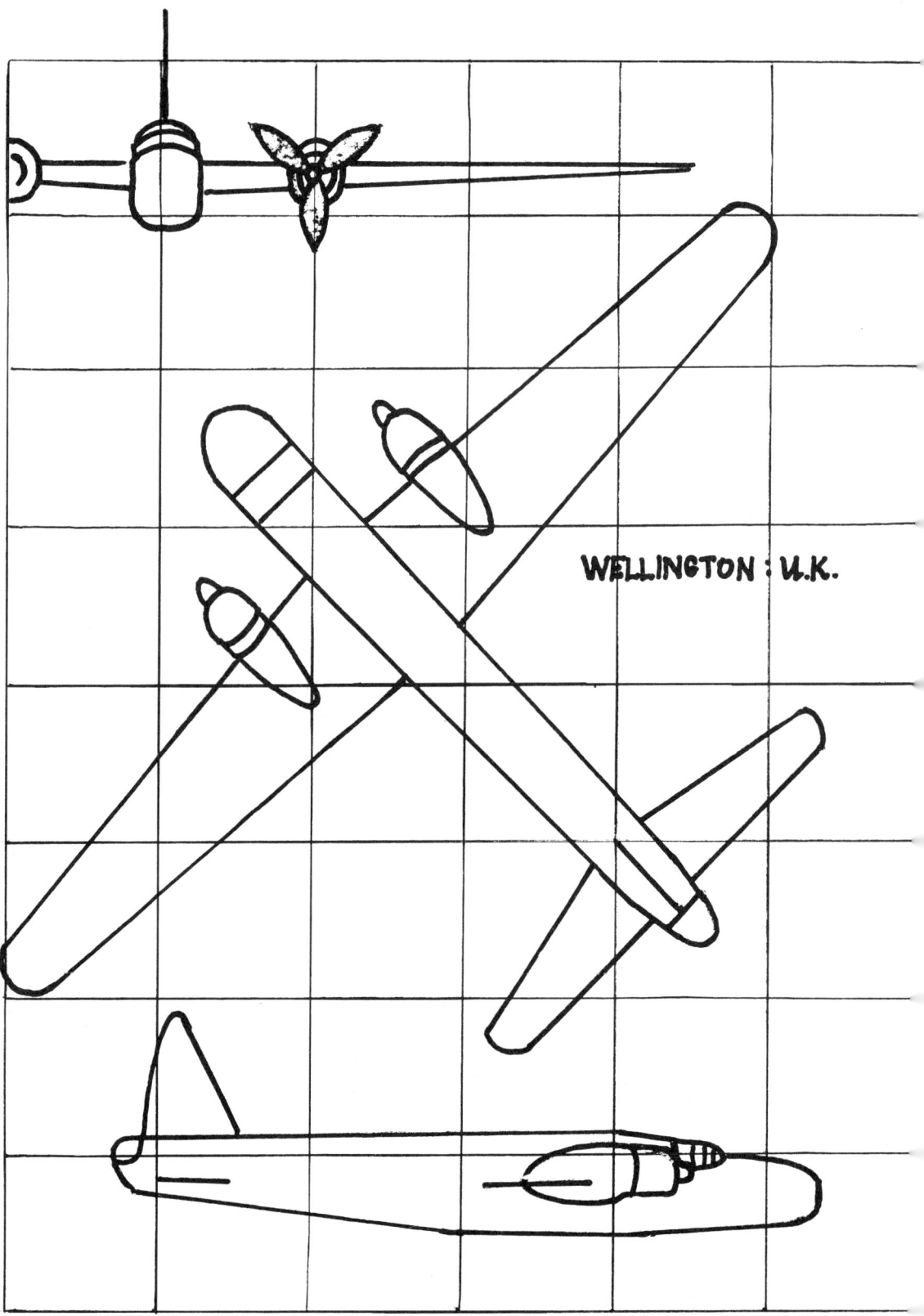

WELLINGTON : U.K.

PLATE 18

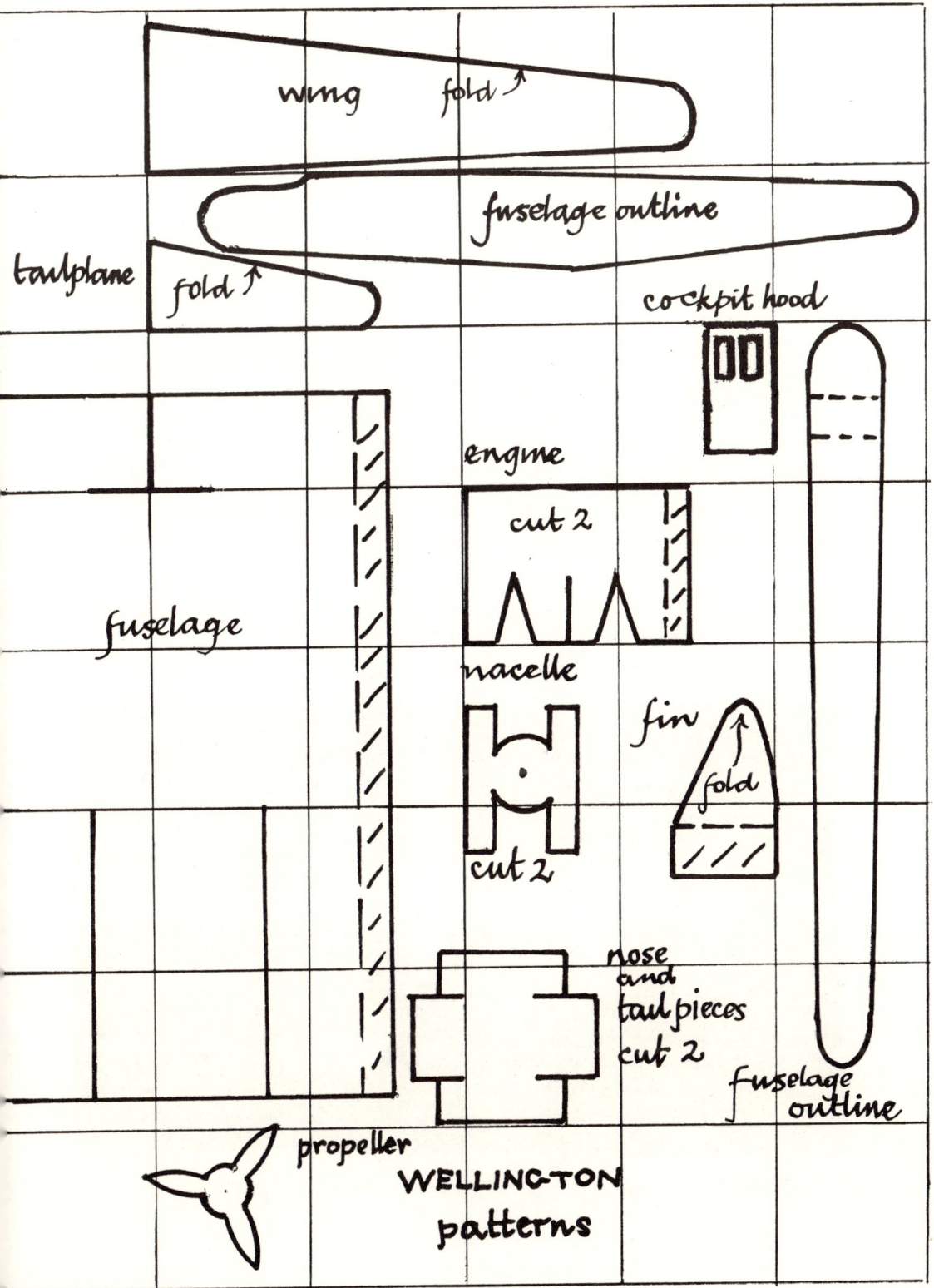

wing fold ↑

fuselage outline

tailplane fold ↑

cockpit hood

engine cut 2

fuselage

nacelle

fin fold

cut 2

nose and tail pieces cut 2

fuselage outline

propeller

WELLINGTON patterns

PLATE 19

Medium bomber, famous, easily recognisable aircraft of World War 2. Used in Battle of the Atlantic, in Middle and Far East and over Germany. When fitted with special apparatus, it was used as a magnetic mine destroyer. Span 85 ft. 2 in.; length 64 ft. 7 in.; maximum speed 247 m.p.h.

Patterns

Trace and cut out fuselage. Make cuts along lines at top front (T form) and at rear of fuselage. Shape to form a tube and glue at shaded portion. Shape rear of fuselage; shape front of fuselage. Cut and fit nose and tail pieces at front and rear of fuselage.

Cut wing, tailplane and fin from double thickness of paper. Make slits in rear of fuselage and glue in fin and tailplane.

Cut wing in half; make slits at bottom of fuselage and glue in each half to meet in centre of fuselage.

Cut out and fit cockpit hood.

Make engines and glue to wing.

Make engine nacelles and glue over engines.

Make and attach propeller with pin. Cover head of pin with tiny cone of paper.

Short Sandringham: U.K. 1945

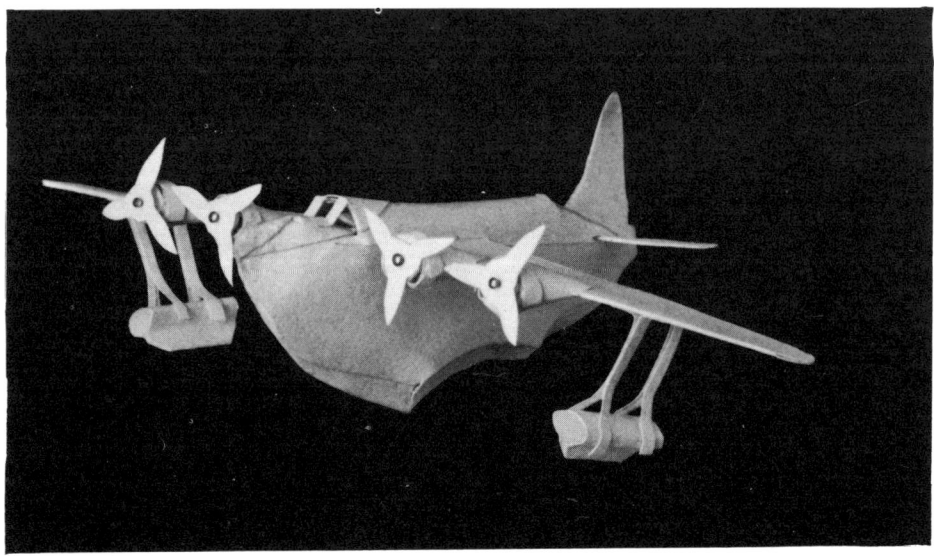

PHOTOGRAPH 9

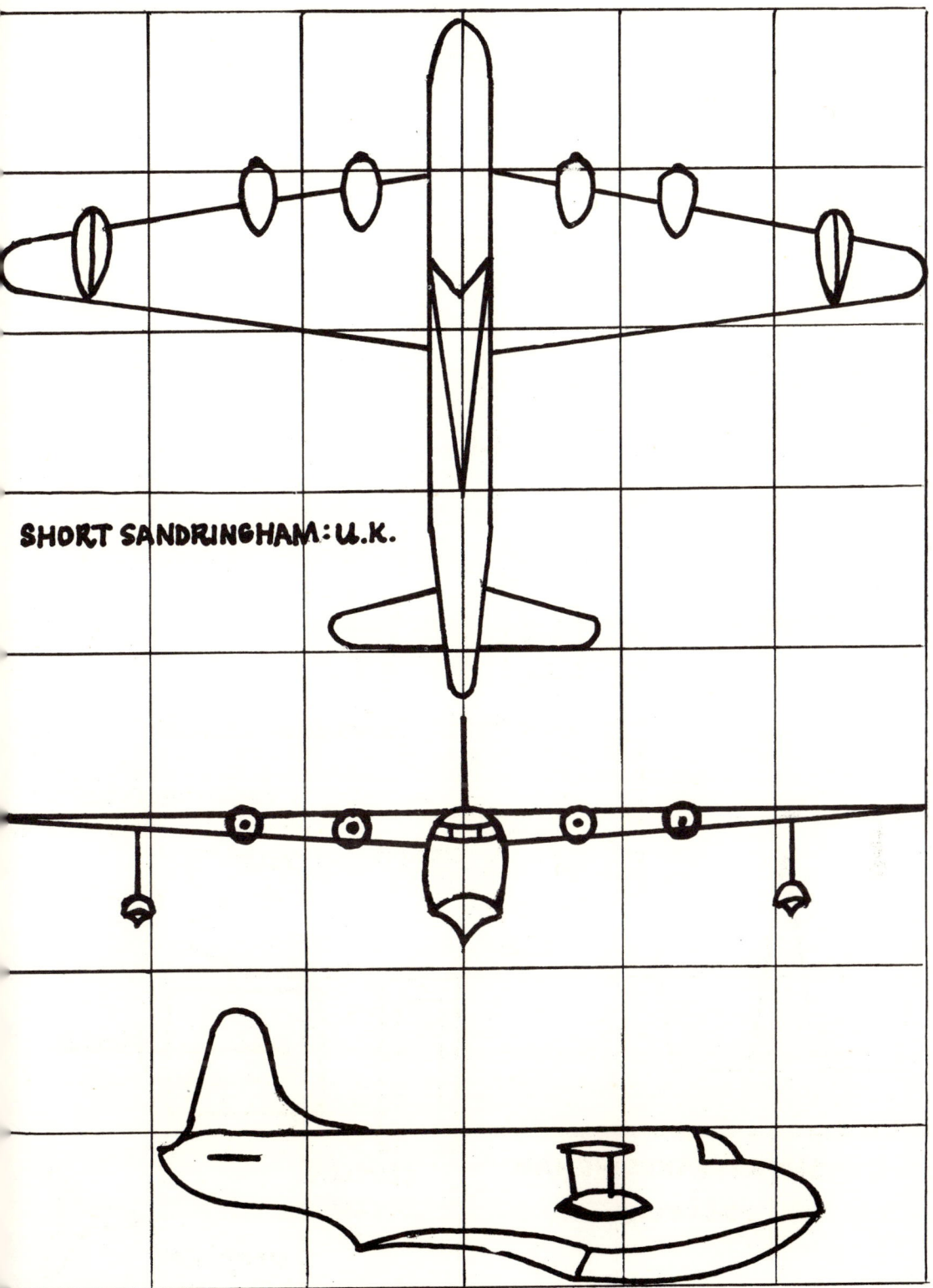

SHORT SANDRINGHAM: U.K.

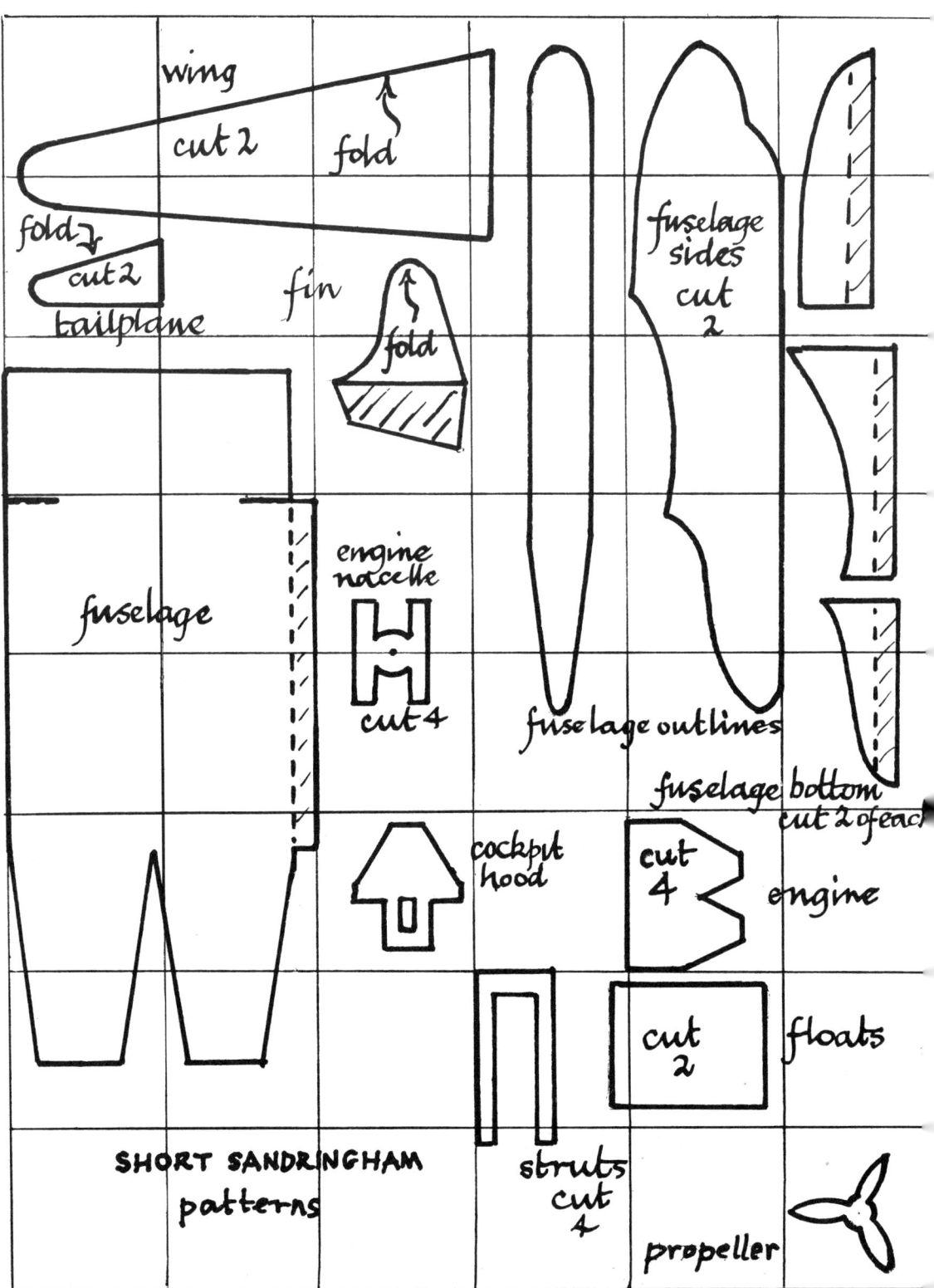

wing

cut 2

fold

fold

cut 2

tailplane

fin

fold

fuselage sides cut 2

fuselage

engine nacelle

cut 4

fuselage outlines

fuselage bottom
cut 2 of each

cockpit hood

cut 4

engine

cut 2

floats

struts cut 4

propeller

SHORT SANDRINGHAM
patterns

PLATE 21

Civil airliner developed from Sunderland reconnaissance flying boat of World War 2. Some still in use in South America. Span 112 ft. 9½ in.; length 86 ft. 3 in.; maximum speed 251 m.p.h.

Patterns

Make wing in halves, using double thickness. Make fin and tailplane also from double thickness.

Make fuselage by first rolling tube shape and gluing at shaded portion. Cut along lines near top of pattern and glue one piece over the other to give nose shape; glue bottom of pattern and shape to a point. Cut out two fuselage sides from single sheet and glue one each side of fuselage tube; cut out fuselage bottom pieces from single sheet and glue shaded portions to bottom of fuselage sides. Join bottom of these pieces with glue to form float shape at bottom of fuselage.

Cut slits at rear of fuselage and glue in fin and tailplane.

Cut and fit cockpit hood over shaped part of nose.

Cut slits in top of fuselage behind cockpit and glue in wing halves: check with Plate 20.

Make floats and join to wing with struts.

Make engines and glue to wing.

Cut and glue nacelles on engines. Pierce small hole for propeller pin in each nacelle.

Cut and fix propellers with pins.

de Havilland Dove: U.K. 1945

Private and business light transport aircraft; also still in use with some airlines for carrying a small number of passengers. Span 57 ft.; length 39 ft. 3 in.; maximum speed 230 m.p.h.

Patterns

Trace and cut wing in two halves, double thickness. Trace and cut fin and tailplane in double thickness.

Cut out fuselage pattern and form into tube, gluing at shaded portion. Cut along lines at top and bottom of pattern: shape and glue to make fuselage nose and tail.

PHOTOGRAPH 10

Cut slits in rear of fuselage. Glue in fin and tailplane.

Cut and glue on cockpit hood.

Make slits at bottom of fuselage for wing. Glue in the two halves to meet inside the fuselage.

Make and fit engines over wing and add nacelles.

Cut out propellers, and fix to nacelles with pins. Make tiny cone to go over head of pins.

DOVE : U.K.

PLATE 22

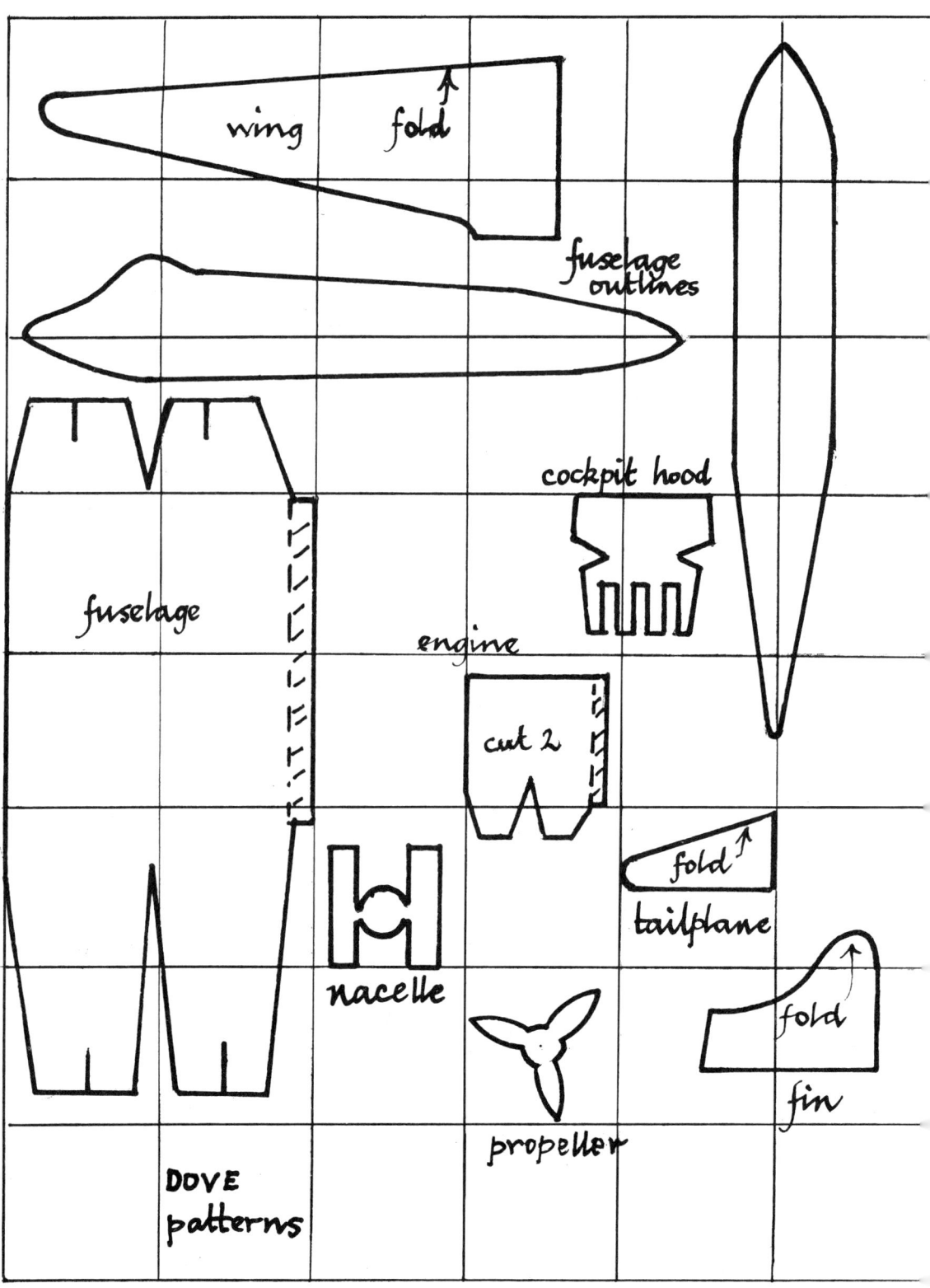

wing fold

fuselage outlines

cockpit hood

fuselage

engine

cut 2

nacelle

tailplane fold

propeller

fin fold

DOVE patterns

PLATE 23

Auster Autocrat: U.K. 1945

Photograph 11

Civil light aeroplane; span 36 ft.; length 23 ft. 5 in.; maximum speed 120 m.p.h.

Trace wing and cut from double thickness with fold on leading edge. Trace and cut out fin and tailplane.

Cut out fuselage pattern. Roll into tube and glue shaded portion. Shape and glue rear of fuselage. Make two small cuts at front of fuselage where shown: glue these to shape front slightly but leave nose open.

Make cockpit hood and glue in position with top flat. Glue wing to top of cockpit hood.

Fix fin and tailplane by making slits in rear of fuselage and gluing them in.

Make and fix struts to wing and fuselage.

Make nacelle to fit over front of fuselage. The oblong sides of the pattern are made into a tube.

Make and fit wheel struts and wheels from double thickness.

59

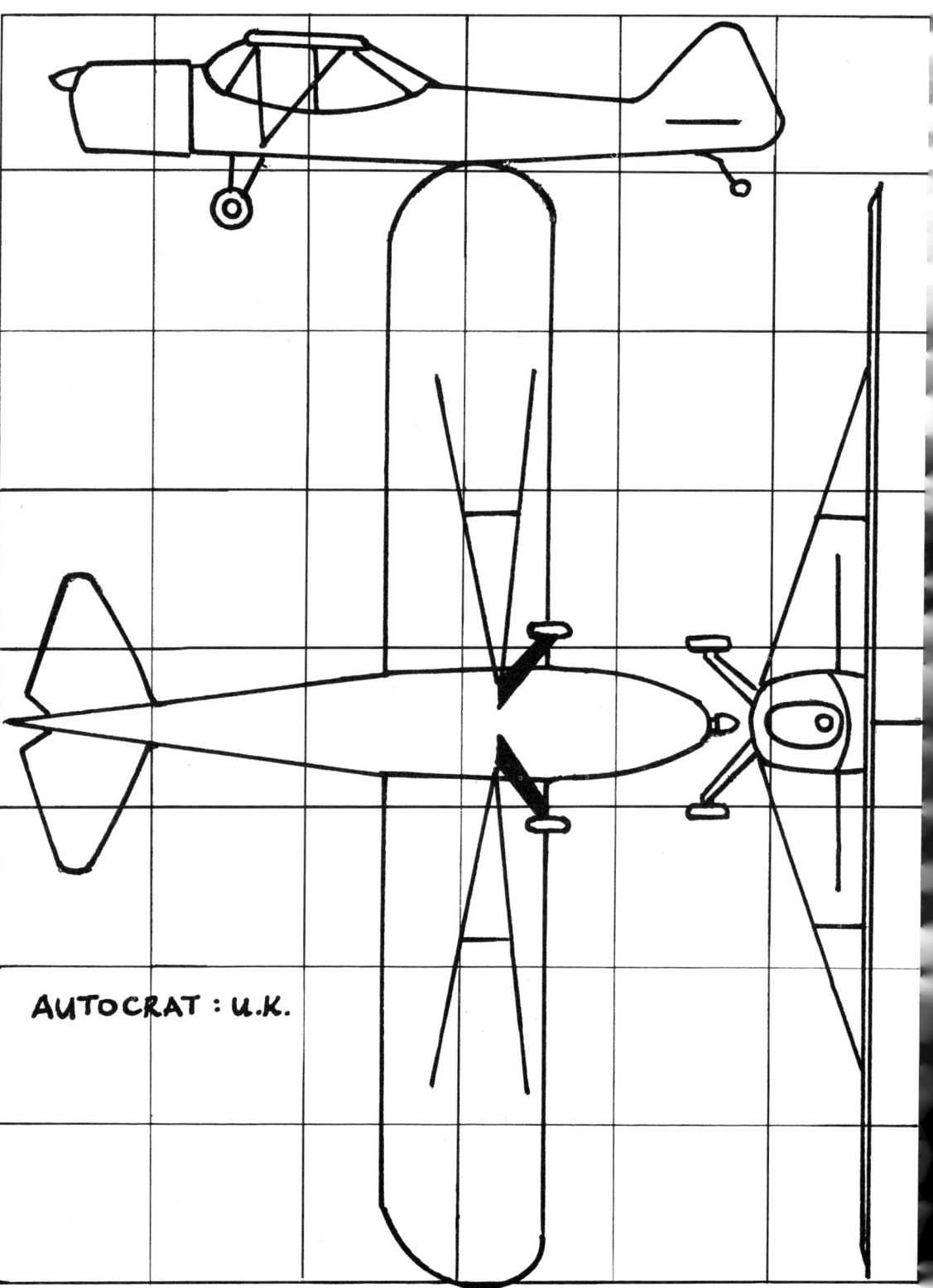

AUTOCRAT : U.K.

PLATE 24

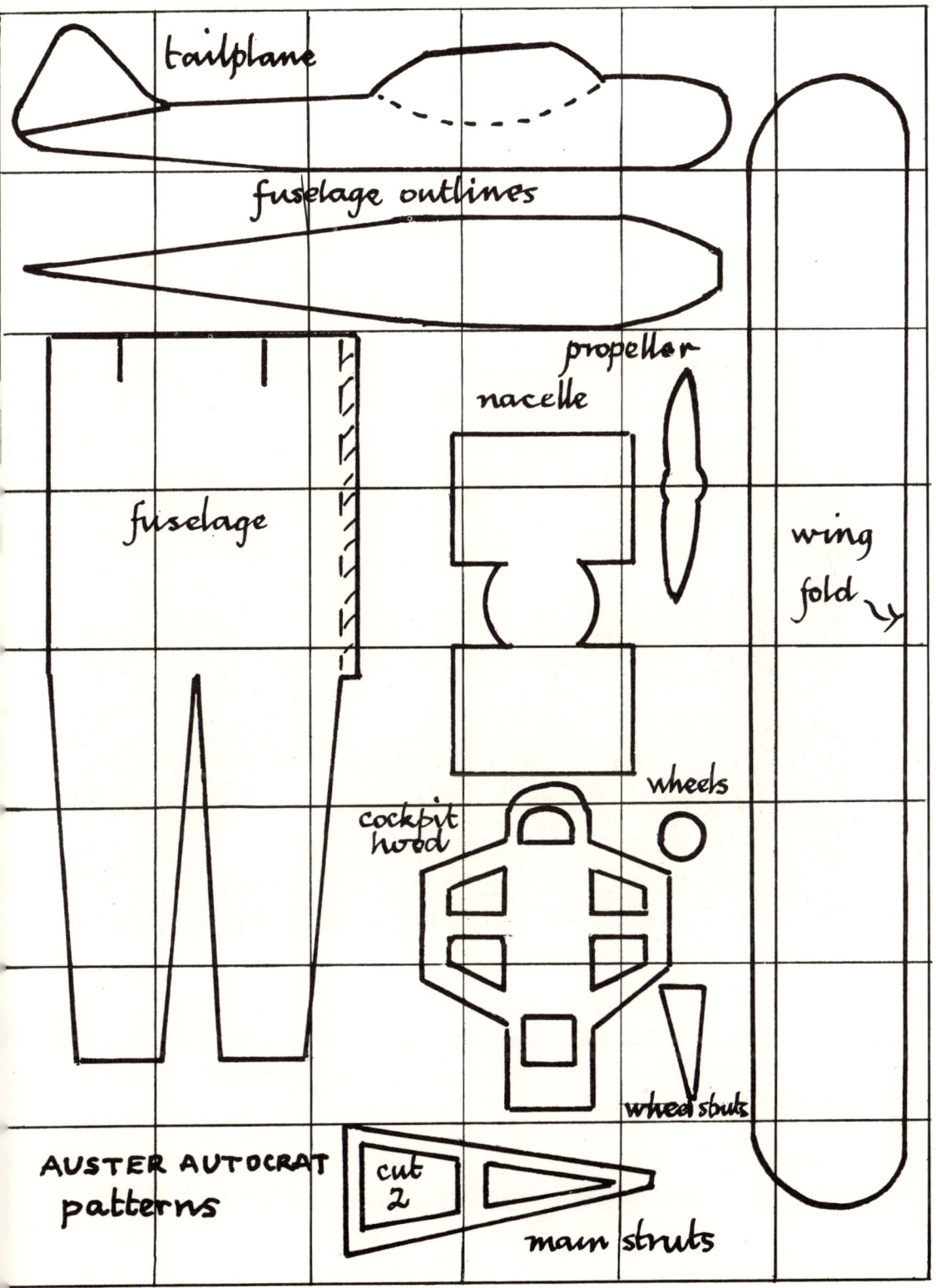

tailplane

fuselage outlines

propeller

nacelle

fuselage

wing
fold

wheels

cockpit
hood

wheel struts

AUSTER AUTOCRAT
patterns

cut
2

main struts

PLATE 25

Make and fit propeller with pin. A tiny tube of paper is fitted between the propeller and nacelle, and a tiny cone is glued on the propeller over the head of the pin.

Pilatus Porter: Switzerland 1959

PHOTOGRAPH 12

General purpose utility aircraft. A reliable plane, which handles well at slow speeds, used for police patrol and flying doctor duties. It can be fitted with skis for mountain rescue work. Span 49 ft. 8 in.; length 33 ft. 5½ in.; maximum speed 145 m.p.h.

Patterns

Trace and cut out fuselage. Roll into tube and glue shaded portion. Shape

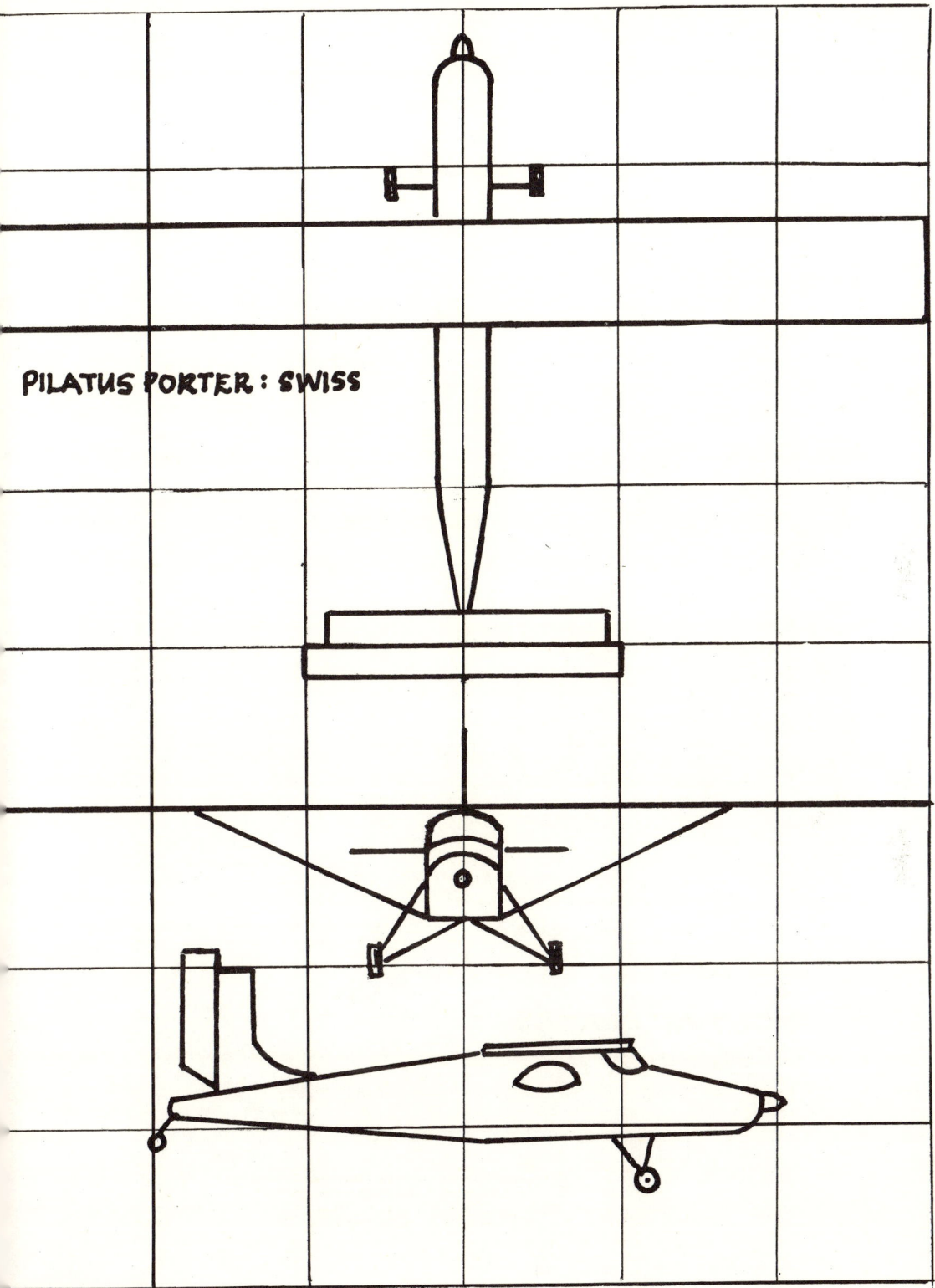

PILATUS PORTER : SWISS

PLATE 26

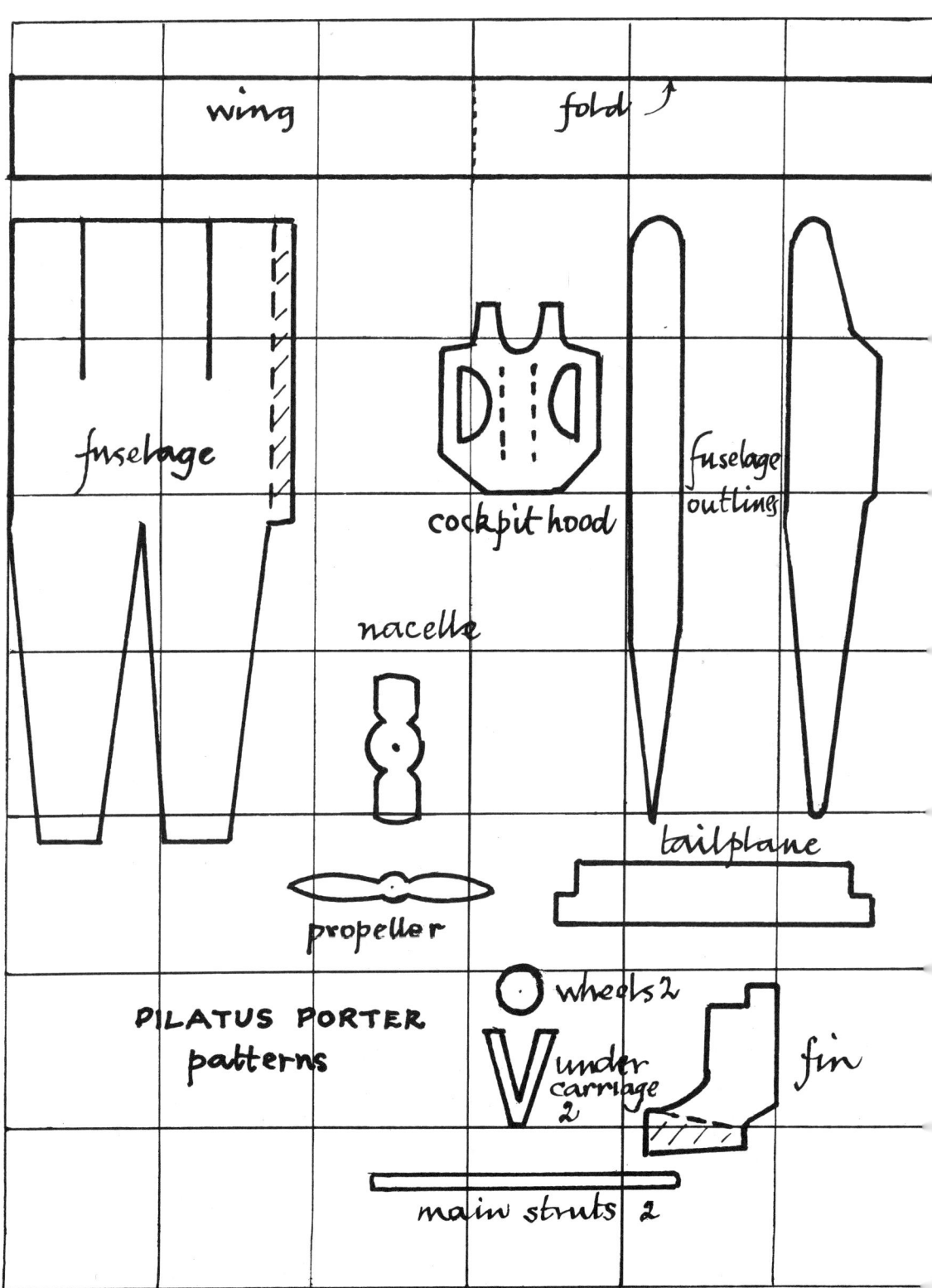

wing   fold ↗

fuselage

cockpit hood

fuselage outline

nacelle

propeller

tailplane

PILATUS PORTER
patterns

wheels 2

under
carriage
2

fin

main struts 2

PLATE 27

rear by gluing tapered edges. Shape front part by cutting along lines and gluing. Leave front open for nacelle.

Cut wing, fin and tailplane from double thickness.

Make cockpit hood. Dotted lines on pattern show where cuts are made to take wing. Fit hood. Cut wing in half and glue in top of hood.

Fit fin. Fit tailplane immediately below fin and on top of fuselage rear.

Make nacelle and fit inside fuselage front.

Make and fit main struts to fuselage and wing.

Make and fit undercarriage and wheels.

Cut out propeller and fix to nacelle with pin with small tube of paper behind propeller. Glue tiny cone of paper to propeller over head of pin. The nacelle can be removed for fixing propeller.

Hawker Siddeley Gnat: U.K. 1959

PHOTOGRAPH 13

Two-seat advanced fighter-trainer. Span 24 ft.; length 31 ft. 9 in.; maximum speed 636 m.p.h.

Patterns

Trace and cut out fuselage pattern – ignore nose pattern. Roll into tube shape and glue shaded portion. Shape rear of fuselage by gluing tapered ends. Trace

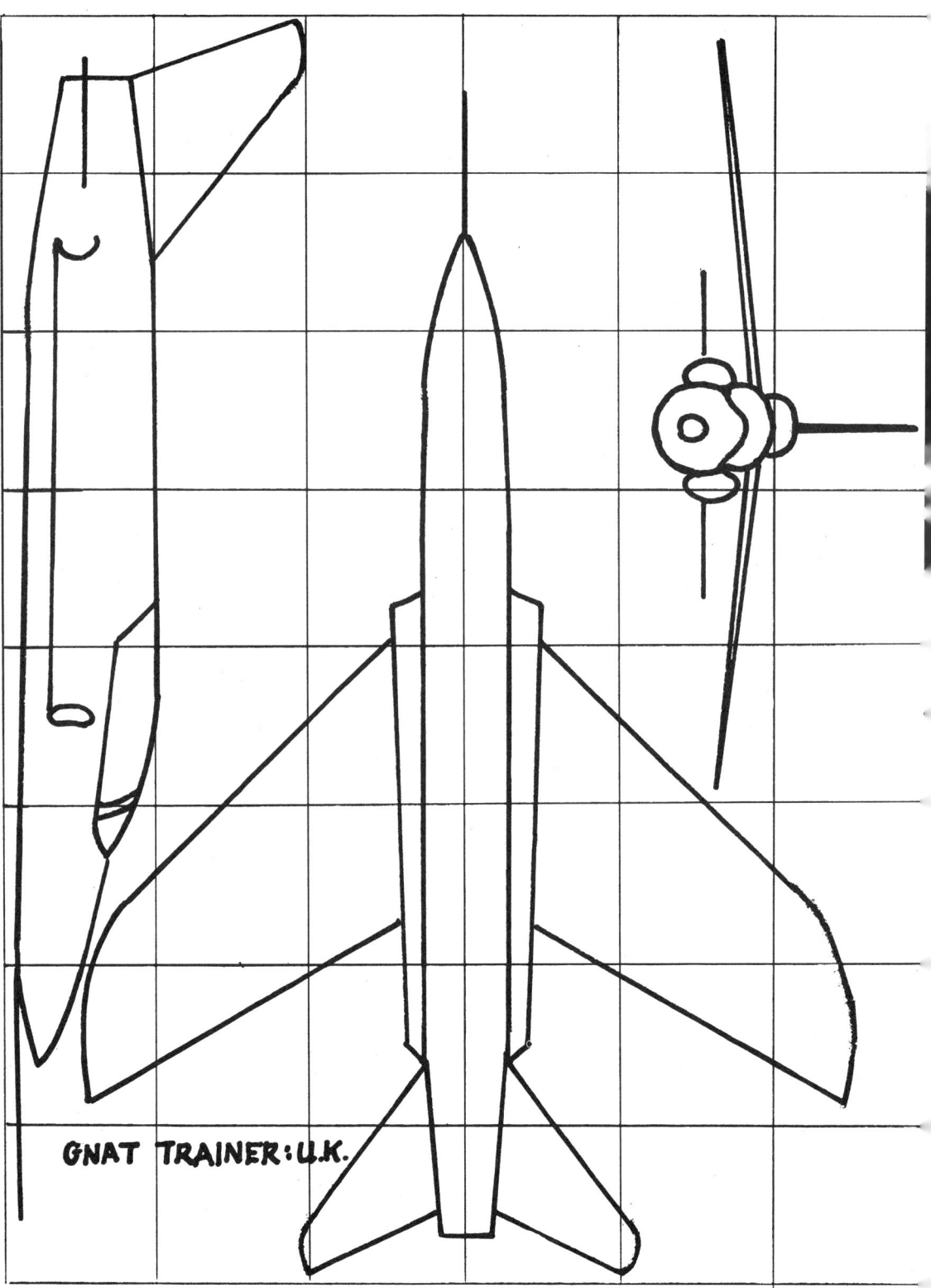

GNAT TRAINER: U.K.

PLATE 28

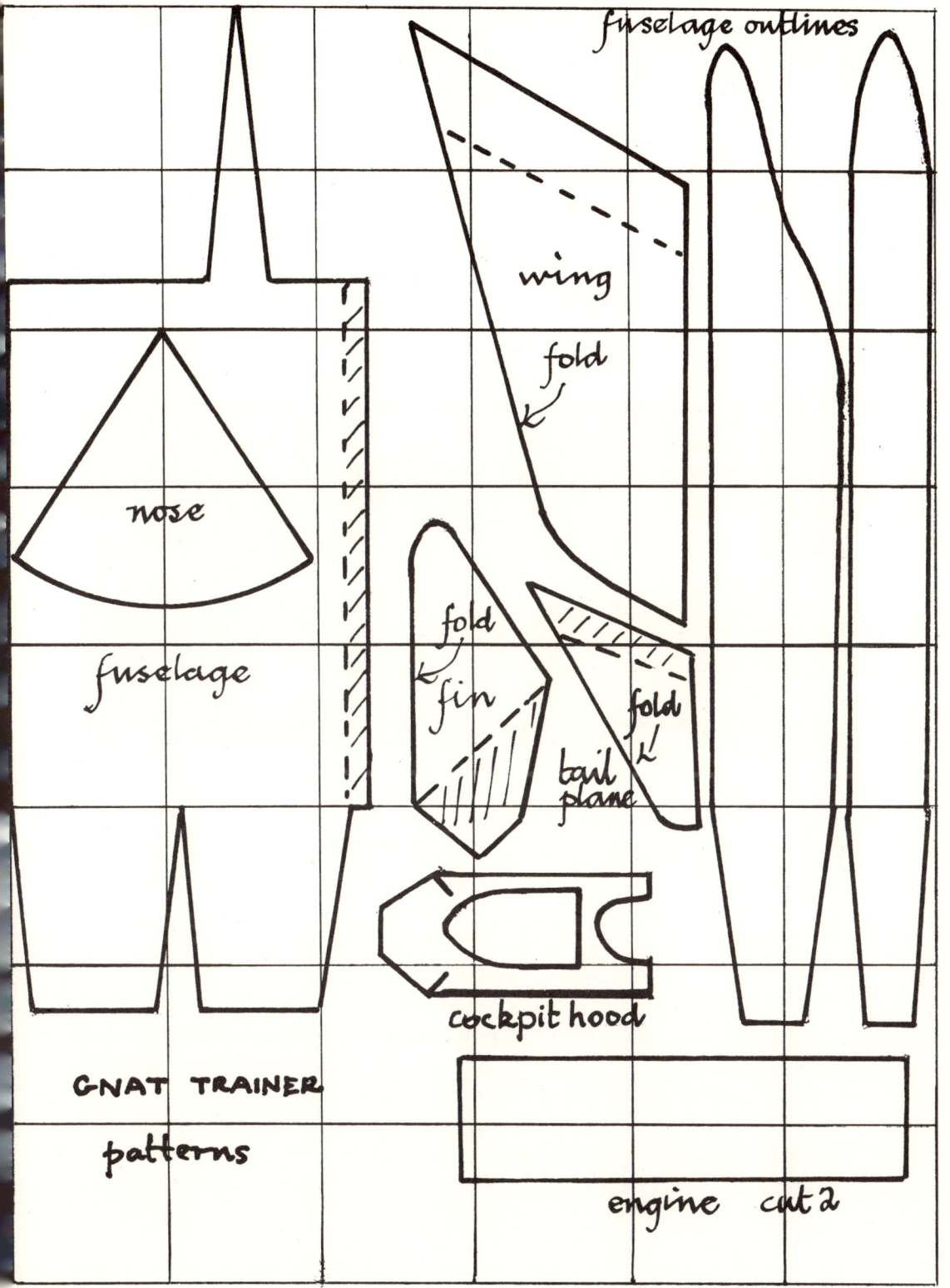

fuselage outlines

wing

fold

nose

fuselage

fold

fin

fold

tail plane

cockpit hood

GNAT TRAINER

patterns

engine cut 2

PLATE 29

and cut out nose pattern and form nose cone from this. Glue nose into front of fuselage with the projecting tab as a support for the length of the bottom of the nose cone. Note that the nose cone slopes downwards.

Cut and fit cockpit hood.

Cut and fit fin and tailplane: cut tailplane in half for fitting.

Cut wing in two halves from double thickness. Dotted lines show how far wing is put inside slits at top of fuselage.

Make and fit engines beneath wing to fuselage and wing.

Fit cocktail stick or something similar as probe.

Mikoyan Midget: U.S.S.R. 1950

PHOTOGRAPH 14

Two-seat advanced fighter-trainer in use in many Communist countries. Span 35 ft. 5 in.; length 36 ft. 1 in.; maximum speed 630 m.p.h.

Patterns

Trace and cut out fuselage. Roll into tube shape. Glue tapered parts to form front and rear of fuselage. Leave ends open.

Cut fin and tailplane from double thickness with fold on leading edges.

Cut wing in two halves from double thickness: dotted lines show part put into slits made at side of fuselage. Glue into fuselage.

Glue fin in slit made in rear of fuselage.

Glue tailplane cut in two halves at top of fin.

Make and fit cockpit hood.

68

MIDGET : U.S.S.R.

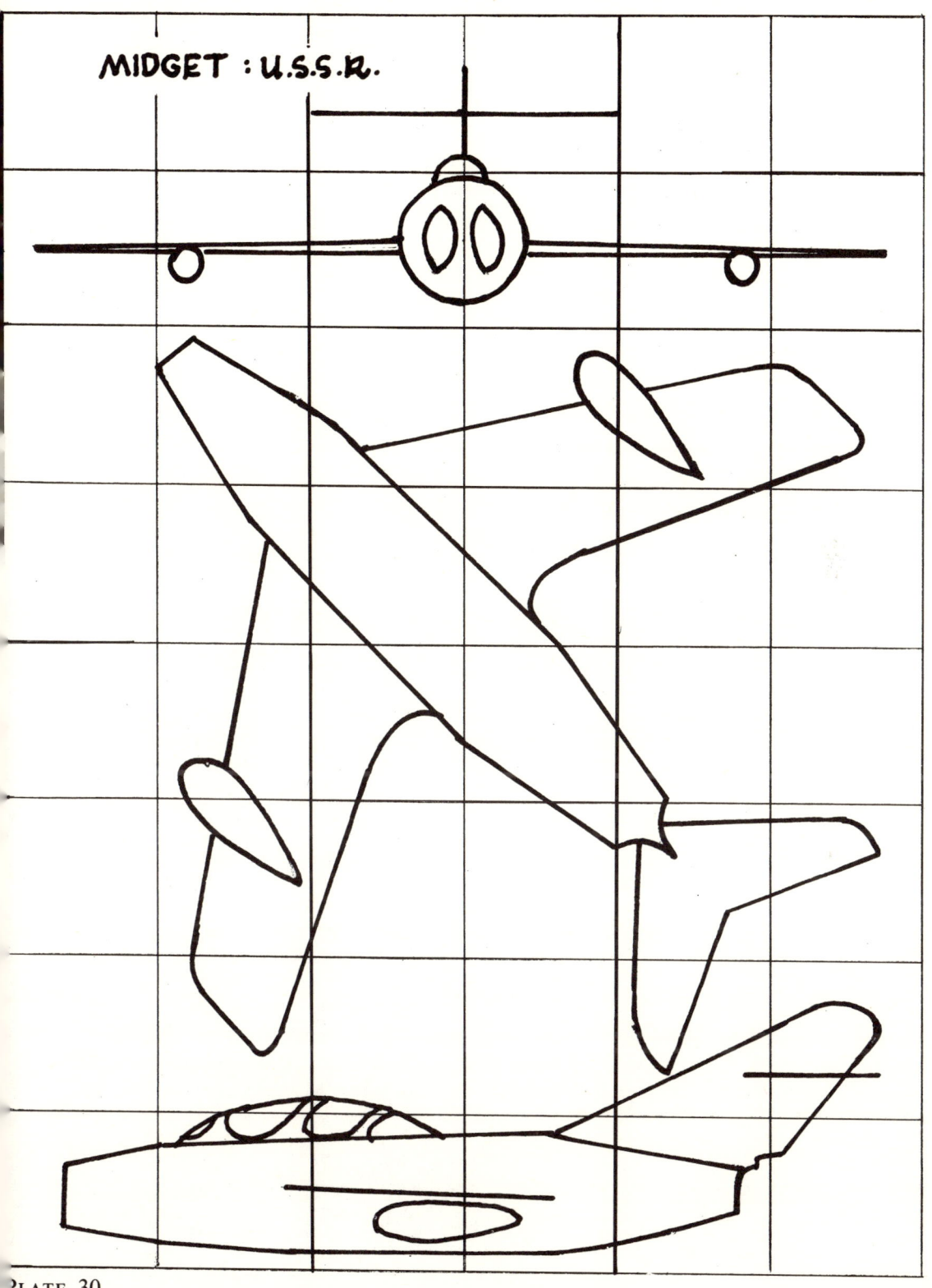

PLATE 30

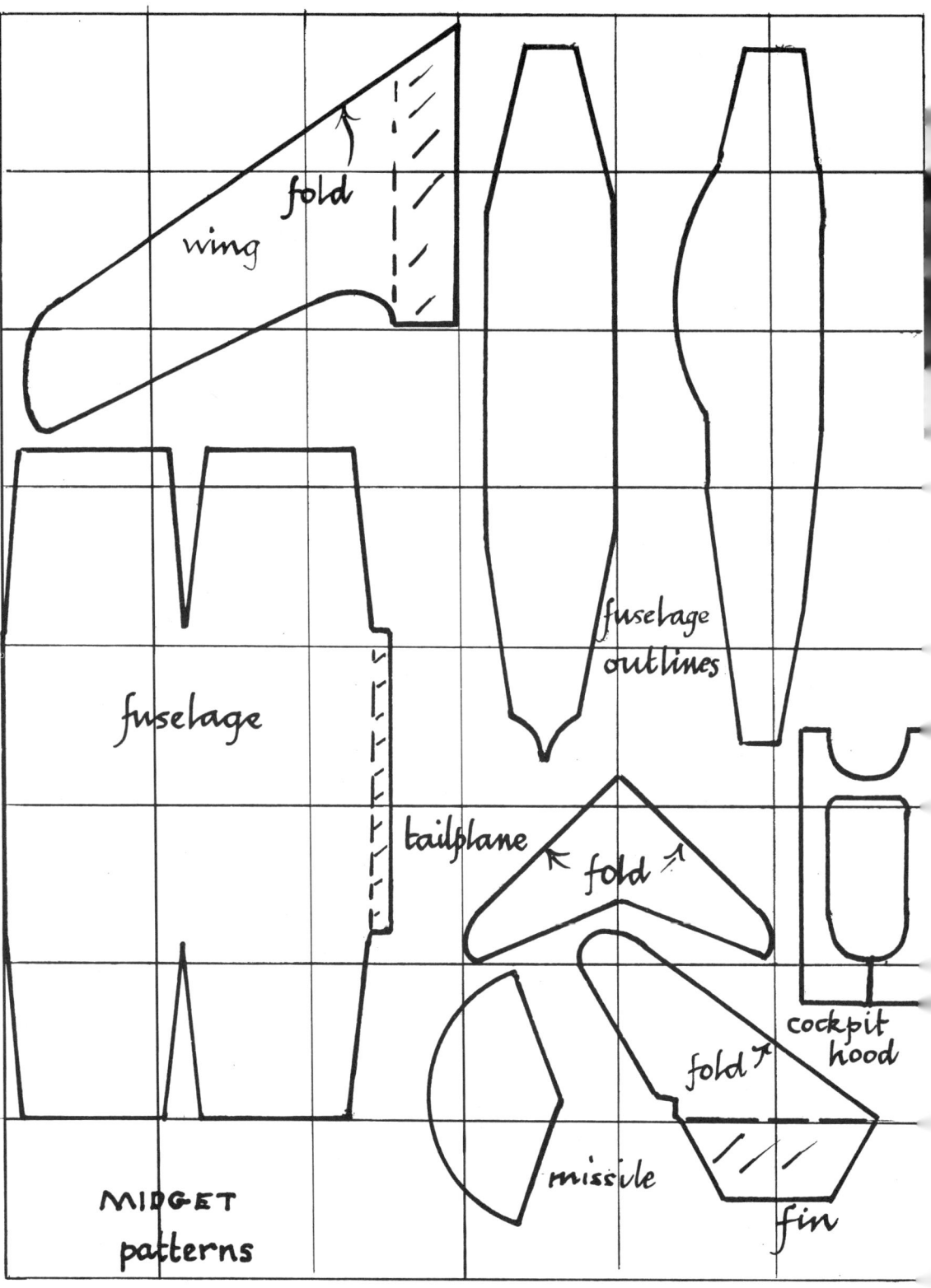

fold

wing

fuselage
outlines

fuselage

tailplane

fold

cockpit
hood

missile

fold

fin

MIDGET
patterns

PLATE 31

Make and fit missiles: make missile pattern into cone and glue small circle of paper over base of cone for missile head. Glue to wing.

Convair Delta Dart: U.S.A. 1961

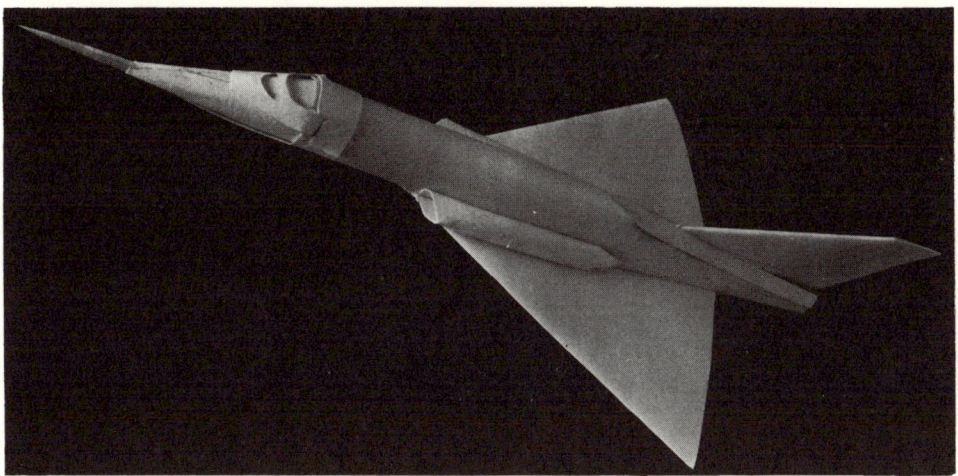

PHOTOGRAPH 15

Single-seat all-weather intercepter-fighter. Span 38 ft. $1\frac{1}{2}$ in.; length with probe 70 ft. $8\frac{3}{4}$ in.; maximum speed 1,525 m.p.h.

Patterns

Trace and cut out fuselage pattern. Roll into a tube shape and glue at shaded portion. Shape rear of fuselage by gluing tapered ends: leave end open. Cut out nose shape and make cone from this. Glue nose cone to projecting tab on fuselage, keeping tab at bottom and using length of tab to support nose cone: note that the cone slopes downwards.

Make wing in two halves from double thickness. Make fin from double thickness. Leading edges must be on fold.

Cut slits for wing at bottom of fuselage and glue halves into these slits. Cut slit for fin at rear of fuselage and glue in fin.

Make and glue on cockpit hood.

Cut two engine patterns. Roll each into a narrow tube. Glue this and close one end. Cut the other end slantwise for head of engine. Glue one engine on top side of wing against the fuselage.

Insert cocktail stick or something similar as nose probe.

71

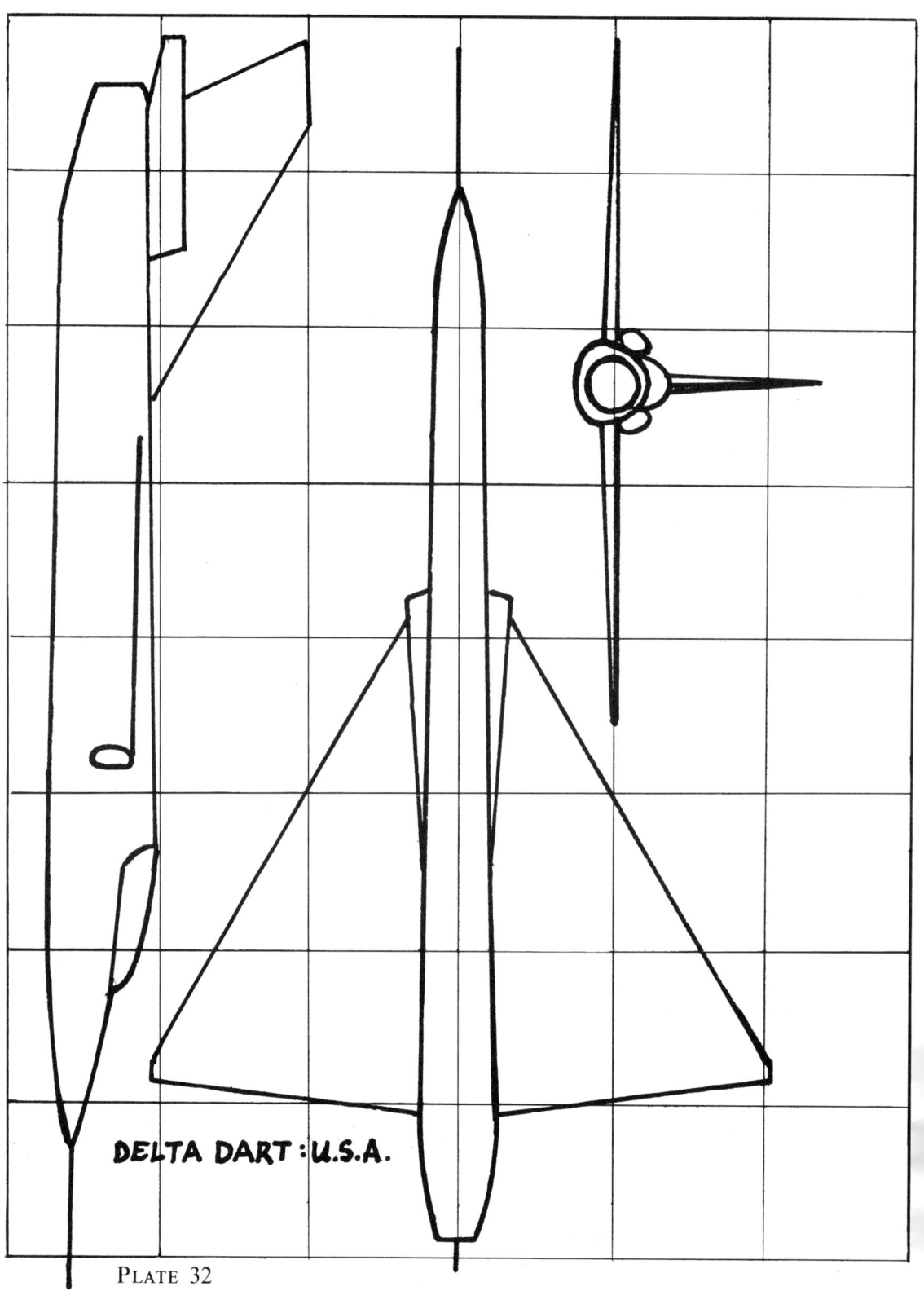

DELTA DART : U.S.A.

PLATE 32

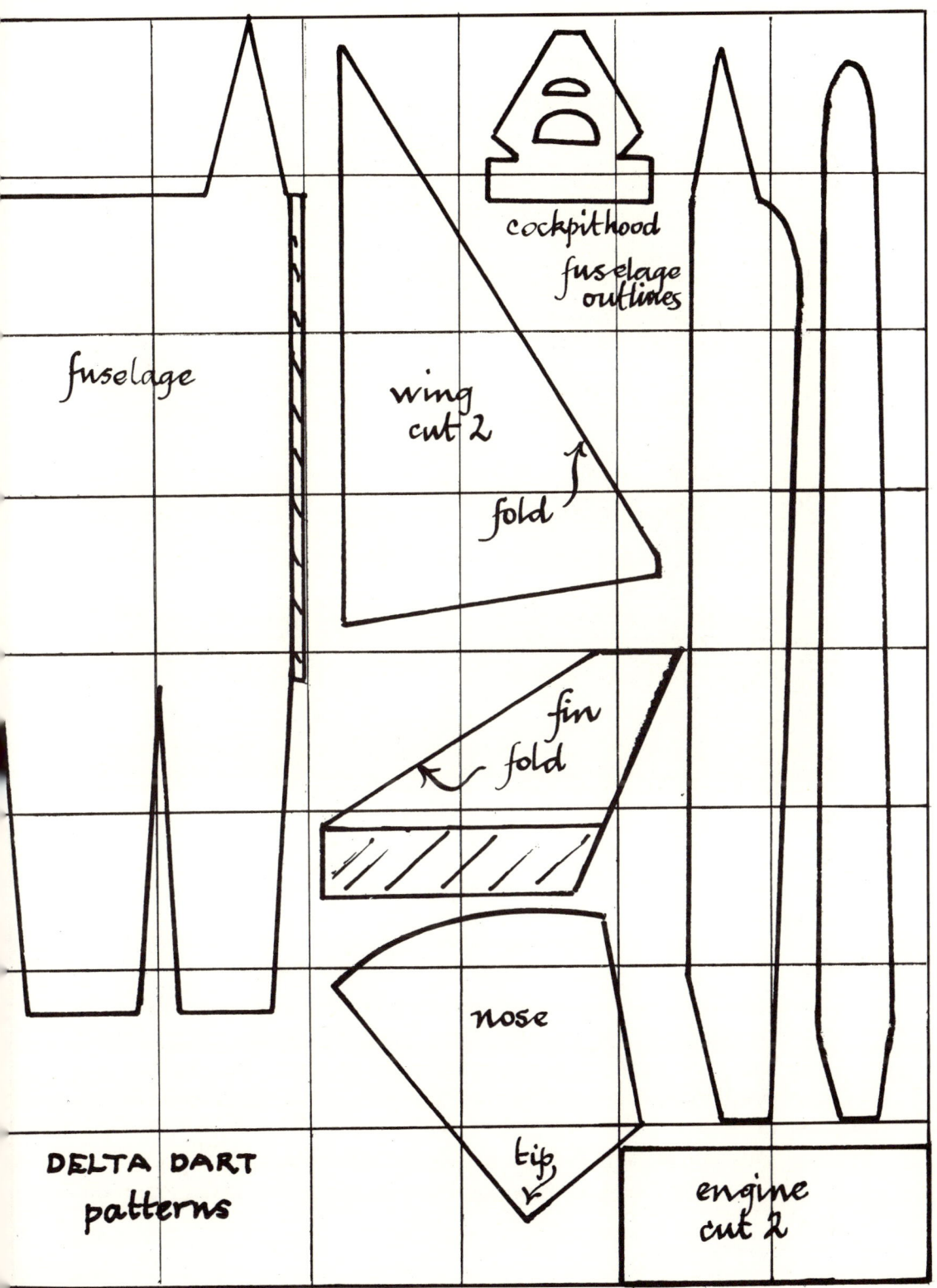

cockpit hood

fuselage
outlines

fuselage

wing
cut 2

fold

fin
fold

nose

tip

DELTA DART
patterns

engine
cut 2

Hawker Siddeley Vulcan: U.K. 1960

PHOTOGRAPH 16

Long-range strike aircraft; the world's largest delta-wing bomber. Span 111 ft.; length 99 ft. 11 in.; maximum speed 645 m.p.h.

Patterns

Cut out and shape fuselage. The oblong pattern is made into a tube into which a nose cone and tail cone are fitted. The cuts on the fuselage pattern, shown by the lines at each end, form tabs for gluing on the cones. Roll the nose and tail pieces to make cones, making sure that they will fit the fuselage before gluing them.

The wings are made in four sections from single thickness of paper. They are glued to the fuselage as shown on Plate 34, that is two to the top of the

74

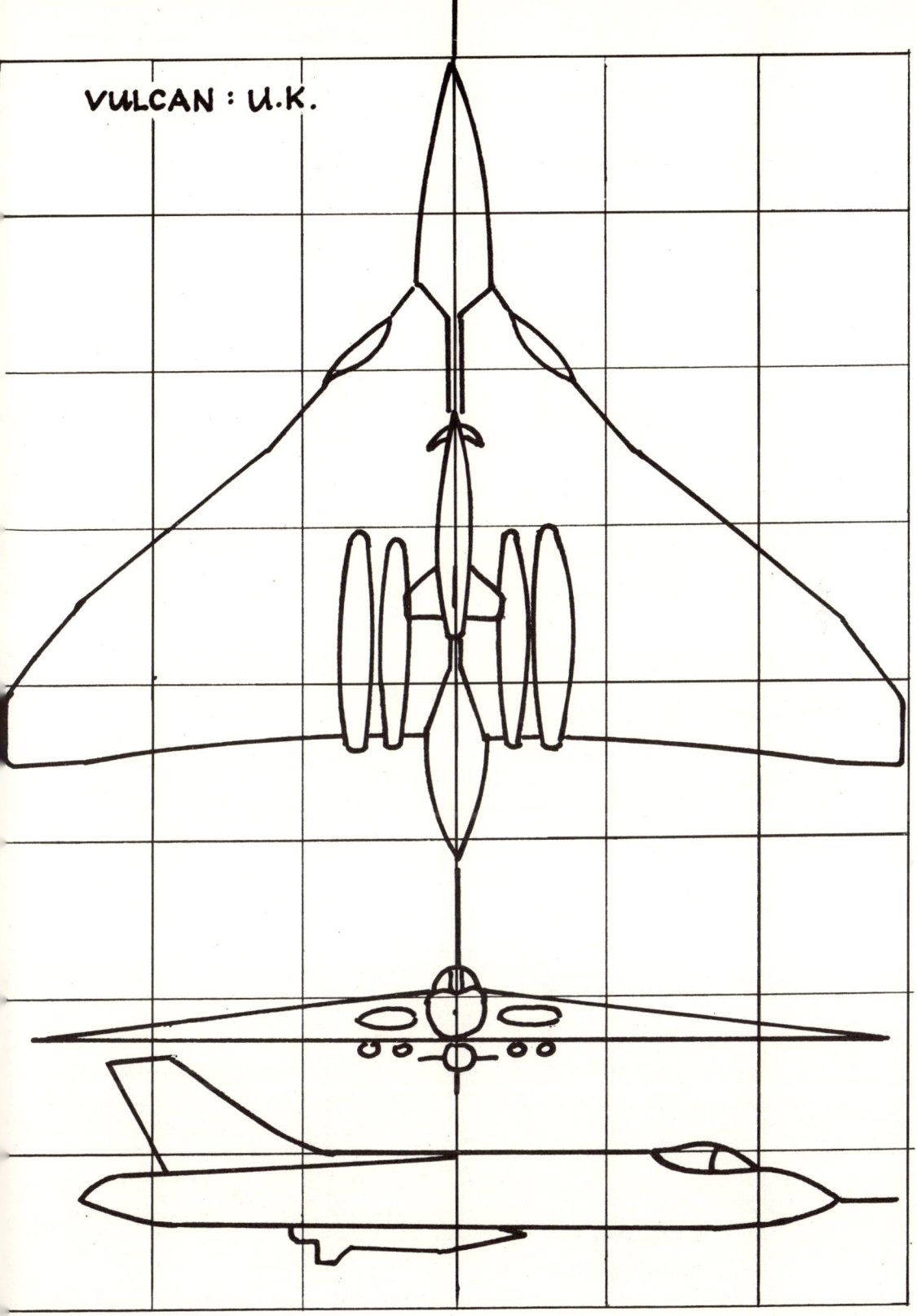

VULCAN : U.K.

PLATE 34

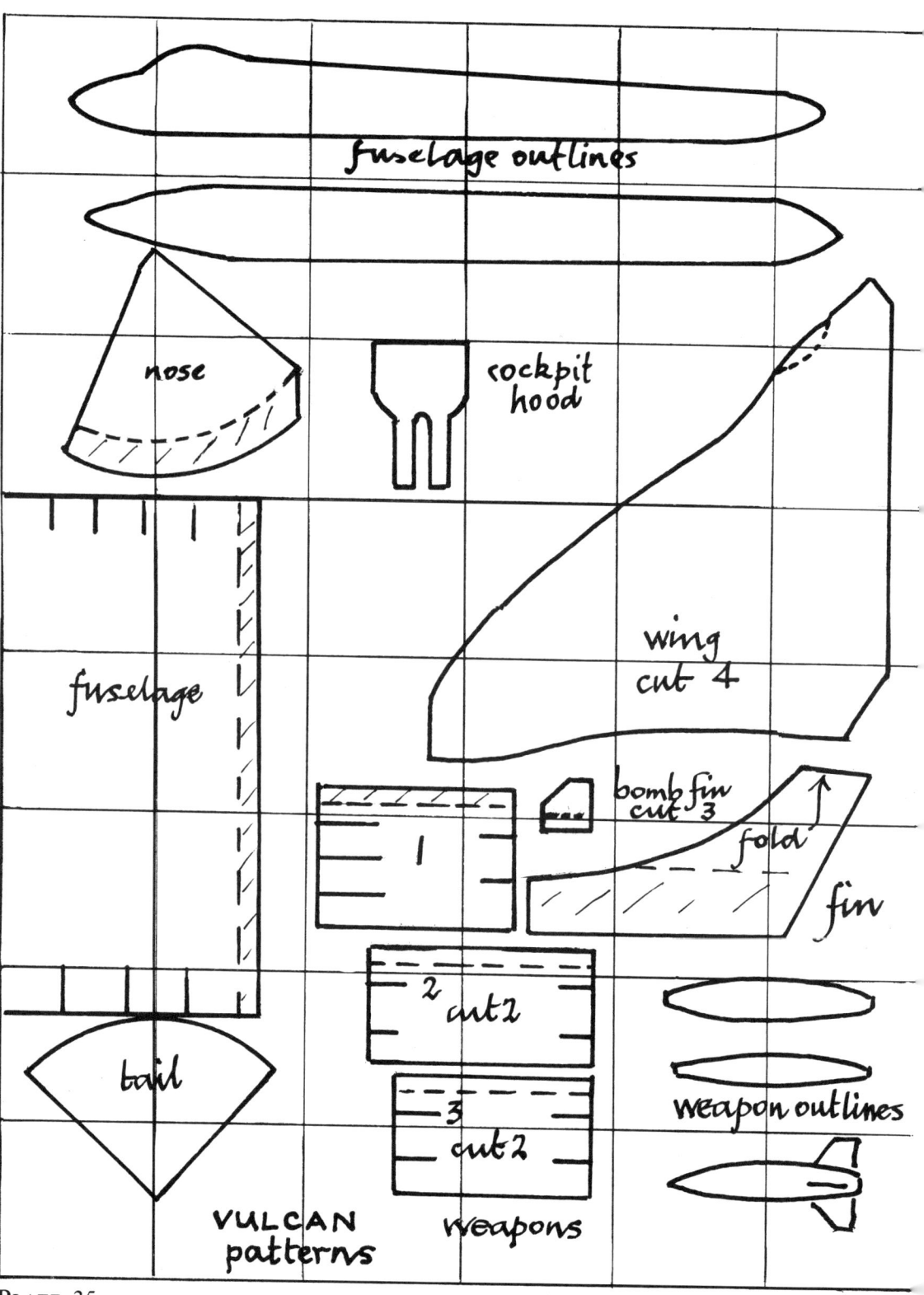

fuselage outlines

nose

cockpit
hood

wing
cut 4

fuselage

bomb fin
cut 3

1

fold

fin

2 cut 2

tail

3 cut 2

weapon outlines

VULCAN
patterns

weapons

PLATE 35

fuselage and two to the bottom. The wings are then sealed with glue round the leading edges only, with a gap, shown by the dotted line, left on each leading edge to represent the engine.

Make the fin from double thickness. Make a slit along the top of the tail to take the fin.

Cut out and attach the cockpit hood. The two prongs become windows and are shaped before the hood is glued in position.

There are two large and two small missiles with a large bomb fixed centrally. Pattern 1 is for the large bomb and the three fins are glued into this. Pattern 2 is for the two large missiles, and pattern 3 for the two small ones. When these are cut out, roll them round a thin piece of dowel to get a tube shape and glue at dotted lines. Small cuts made at each end of a tube will help to get the required shape. They are then glued in position under the aircraft.

Insert a cocktail stick or something similar as a probe.

Douglas Skyhawk: U.S.A. 1954

P HOTOGRAPH 17

Single-seat attack bomber; carries two Bullpup missiles under wing. Span 27 ft. 6 in.; length with probe 42 ft. $10\frac{3}{4}$ in.; maximum speed 685 m.p.h.

Patterns

Trace and cut out fuselage; ignore nose pattern. Roll into tube and glue shaded part. Shape rear of fuselage by gluing tapered ends. Shape front

77

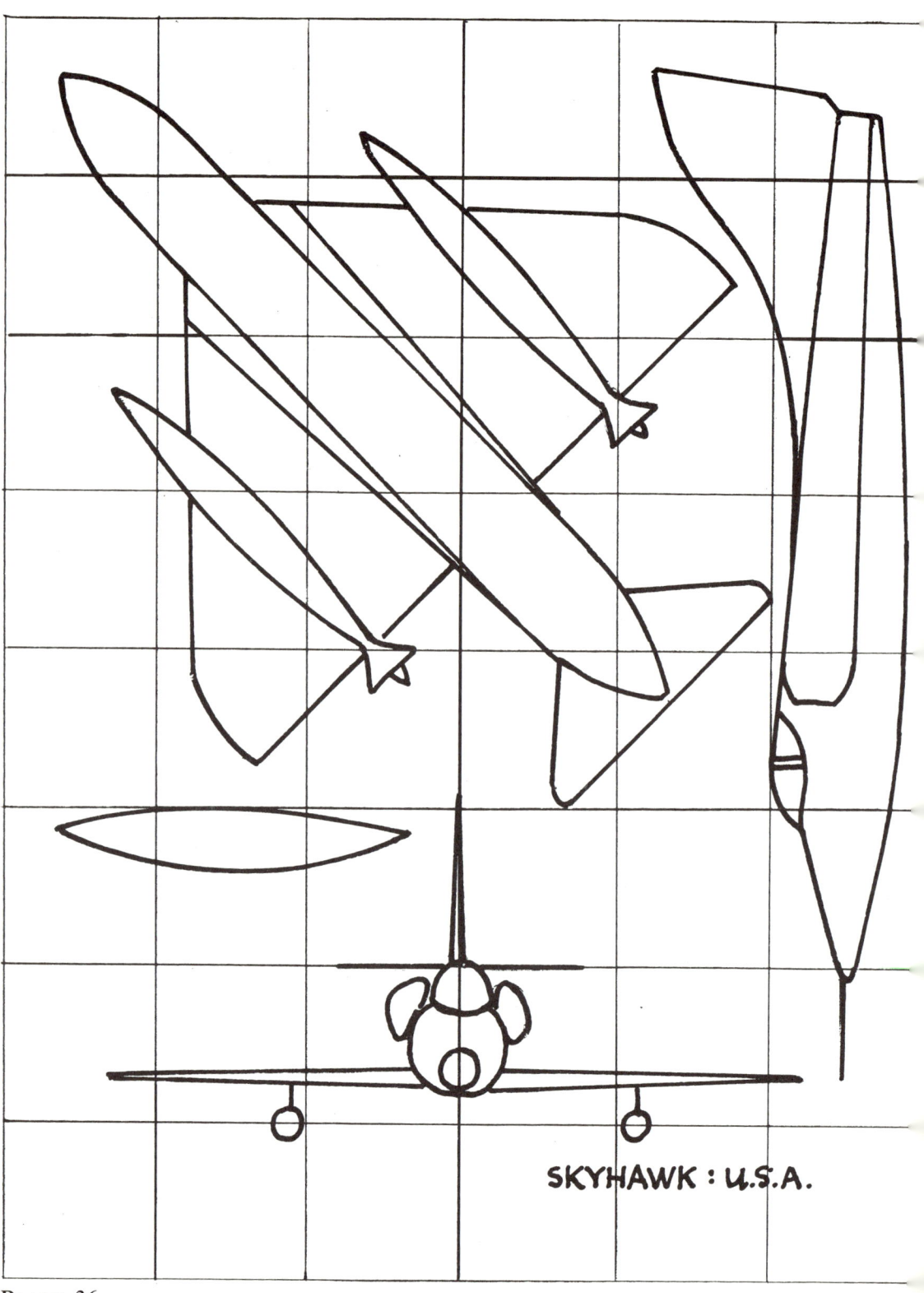

SKYHAWK : U.S.A.

PLATE 36

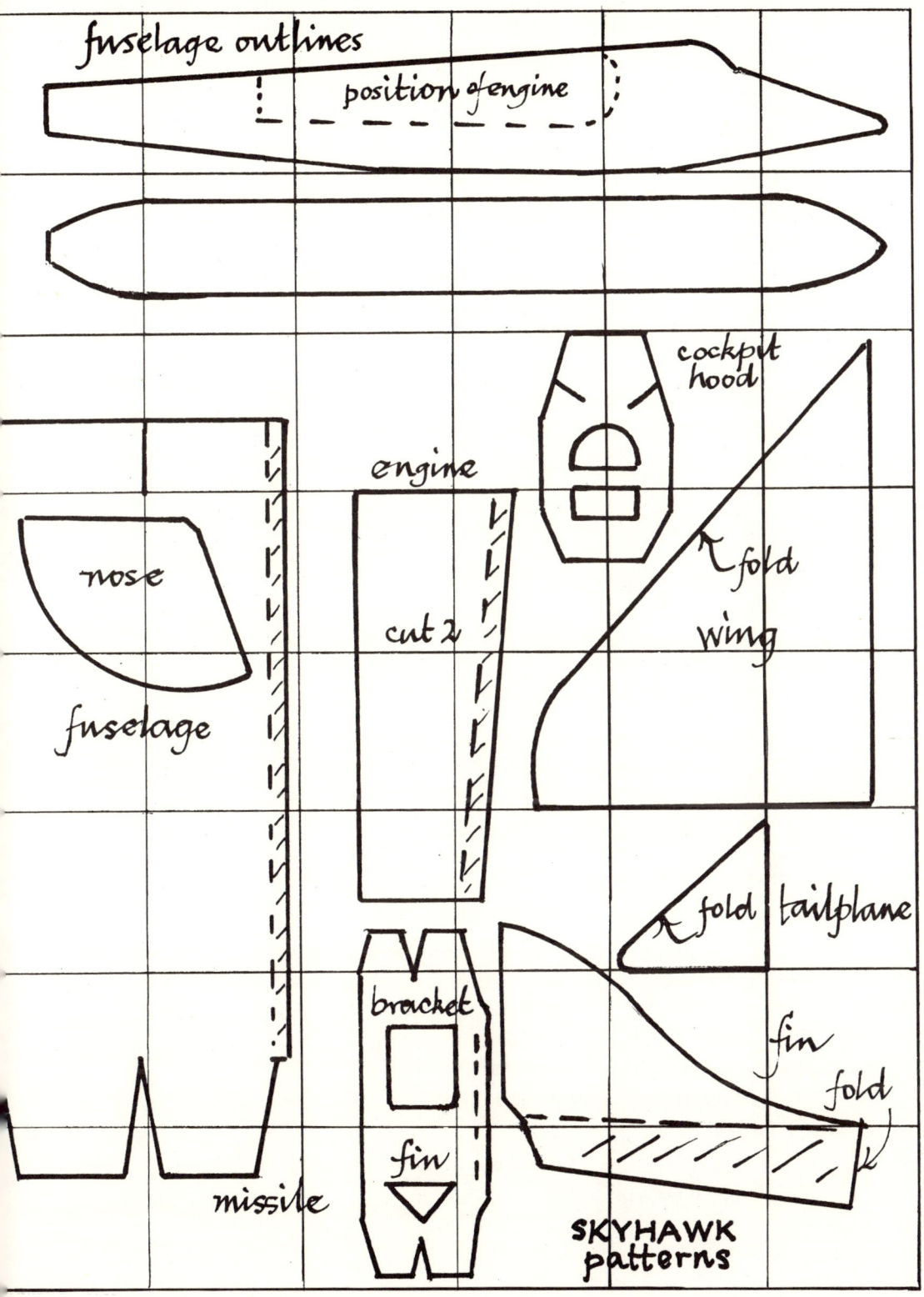

fuselage outlines

position of engine

cockpit hood

nose

fuselage

engine

cut 2

fold

wing

fold tailplane

bracket

fin fold

fin

missile

SKYHAWK patterns

PLATE 37

slightly by gluing at cut. Leave both ends open. Cut nose pattern and make into cone shape to fit front of fuselage. Glue in nose cone.

Cut wing in two halves from double thickness, keeping fold on leading edge.

Make fin and tailplane from double thickness: the tailplane is made in two halves.

Fix fin by cutting slit at rear of fuselage. The tailplane halves are glued on the fin where it touches the fuselage.

Make slits at bottom of fuselage and glue in wing halves.

Make engines: cut out two patterns and roll each into a narrow tube thinner at one end. Glue engine to fuselage and to top of wing: wider ends of tubes face front.

Cut and fit cockpit hood.

Trace and cut out two missile patterns. Roll into tubes and point each by gluing tapered parts: ignore fin and bracket patterns.

Cut two fin patterns and glue one in each missile.

Cut four bracket patterns. These make two brackets. Glue two of each pattern together in middle only and open out to make an H shape. The missiles are glued to the wing with these H brackets.

A probe is made from a cocktail stick and is pushed into the side of fuselage where cone is glued.

Ilyushin Beagle: U.S.S.R. 1947

Light tactical jet bomber. Still used widely in Communist countries. Span 64 ft.; length 58 ft; maximum speed 580 m.p.h.

Patterns

Trace and cut out fuselage. Roll into tube and glue at shaded portion. Shape fuselage at each end by gluing tapered parts. Leave rear slightly open, and front open sufficiently to take the nose cone. Make nose cone from pattern; but note that bottom of nose slopes upwards, when gluing in position.

Cut wing in two halves, tailplane in two halves and fin: all from double thickness.

Make slit at rear of fuselage and glue in fin. The tailplane halves are glued to the fin just above the fuselage.

Make slits in fuselage just above centre and glue in wing halves.

Make and fit cockpit hood.

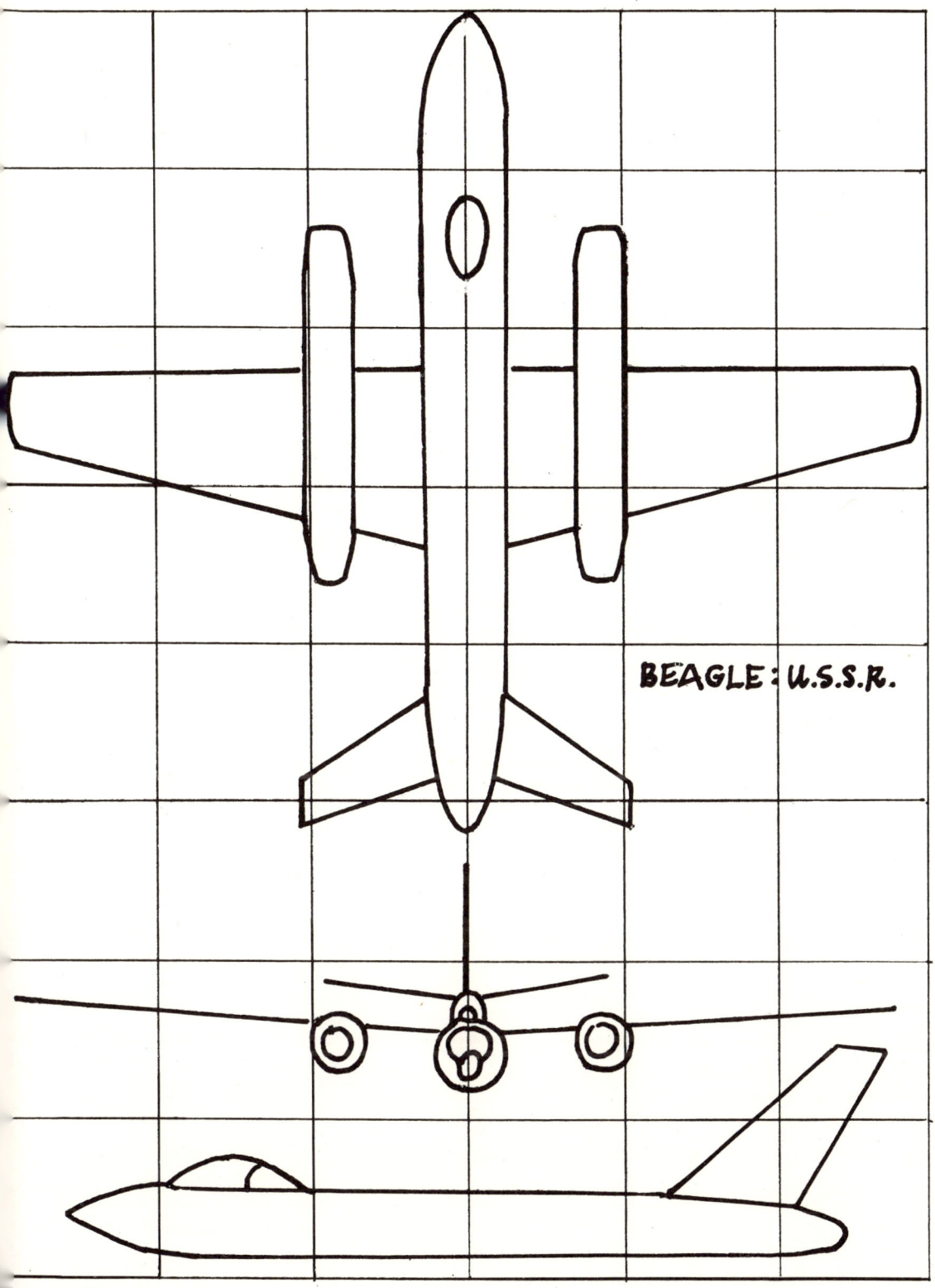

BEAGLE: U.S.S.R.

PLATE 38

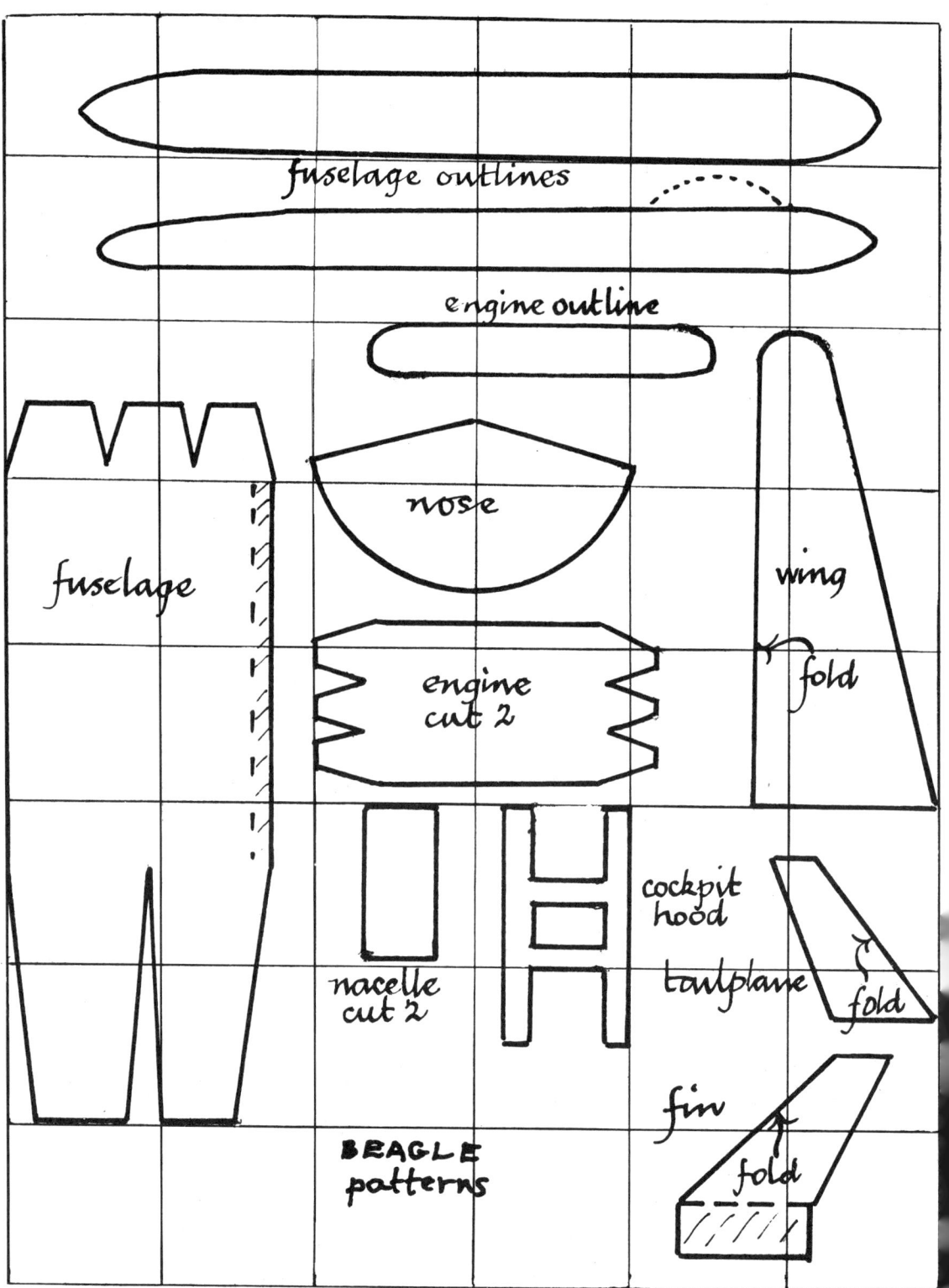

fuselage outlines

engine outline

nose

fuselage

wing

fold

engine
cut 2

cockpit
hood

nacelle
cut 2

tailplane

fold

fin

fold

BEAGLE
patterns

PLATE 39

PHOTOGRAPH 18

Cut two engine shapes and roll into tubes. Taper ends of the engines by gluing tapered parts: leave ends open. Make two nacelles, each a small tube which fits over the front of the engines. Glue engines beneath wing.

de Havilland Comet 2: U.K. 1953

Civil airliner. Span 115 ft.; length 93 ft. $1\frac{3}{4}$ in.; maximum speed 508 m.p.h.

Patterns

Trace and cut out fuselage pattern, making cuts at front. Roll into a tube and glue at shaded portion. Shape rear of fuselage by gluing tapered ends. Shape front by gluing cut parts together, but leave front open sufficiently to take nose piece. Make nose piece and glue in front of fuselage.

83

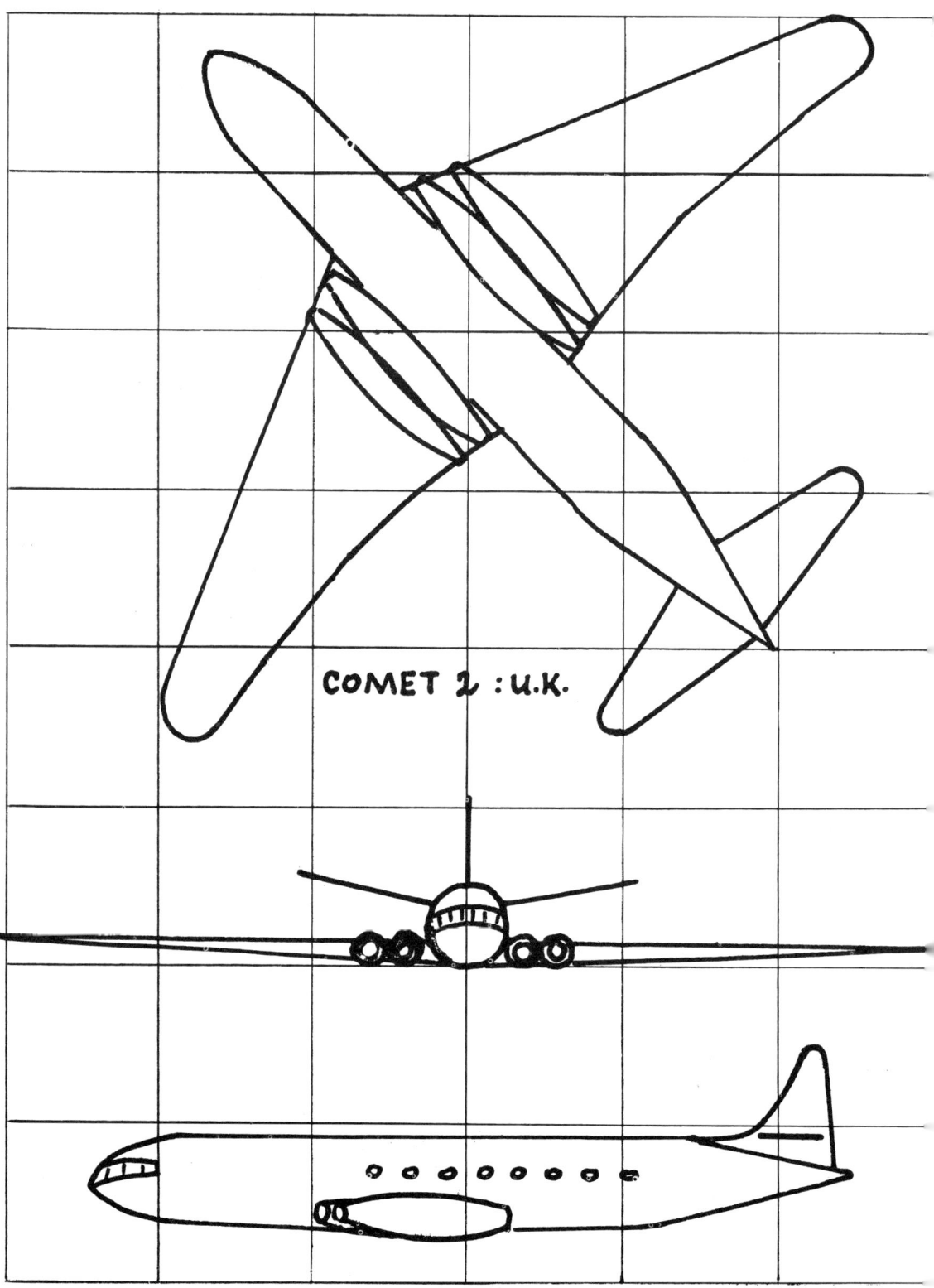

COMET 2 : U.K.

PLATE 40

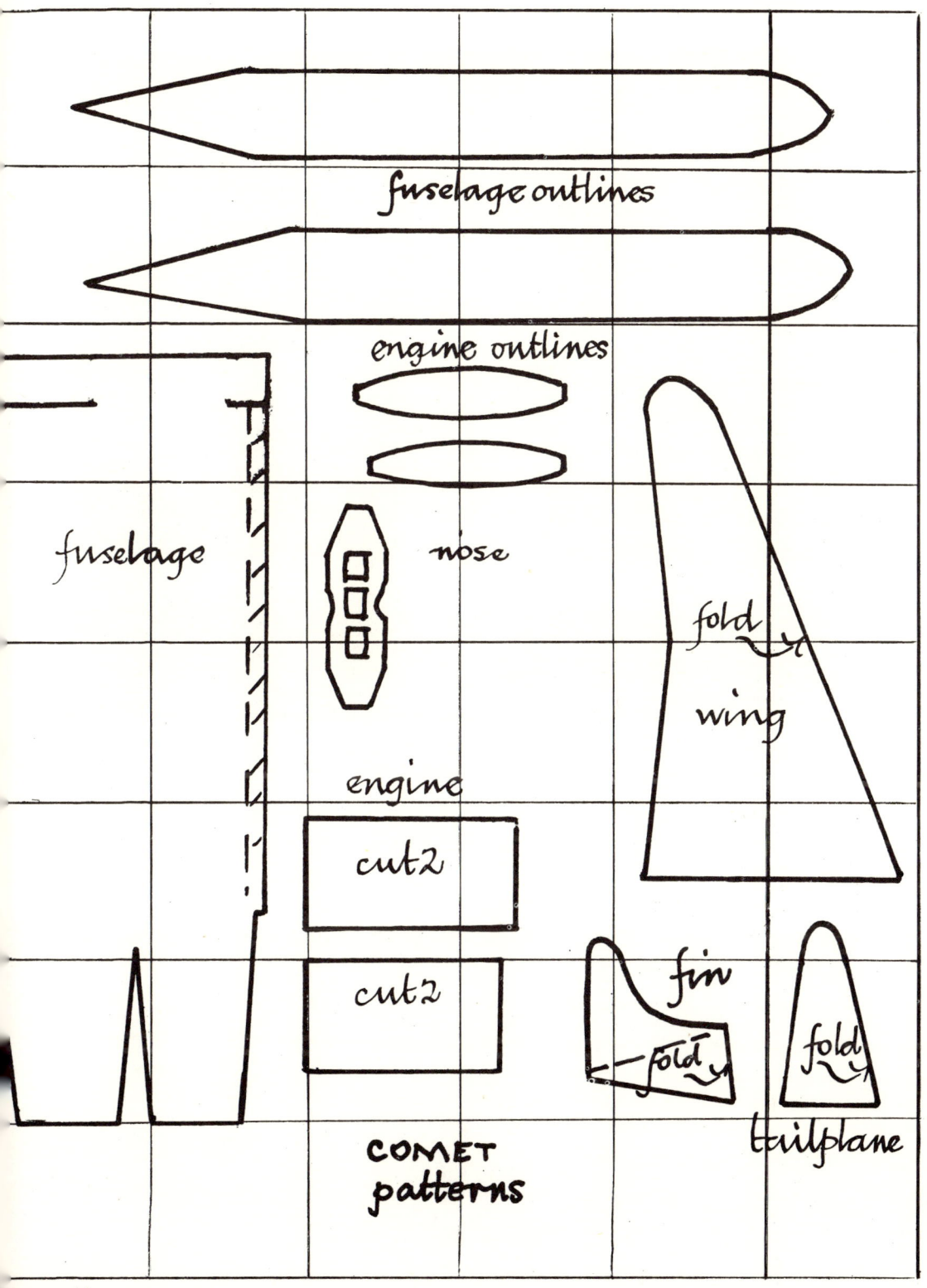

fuselage outlines

engine outlines

fuselage

nose

fold

wing

engine

cut 2

cut 2

fin

fold

fold

tailplane

COMET
patterns

Cut wing and tailplane in two halves; cut fin. All from double thickness.

Make slit at rear of fuselage and glue in fin. Glue tailplane halves on fin just above fuselage.

Cut two of each size engines. Roll into tubes. Cut each tube in half lengthwise: glue one half to top, one to bottom of wing with the larger engine inside against the fuselage.

Sud Aviation Caravelle: France 1955

PHOTOGRAPH 20

Civil airliner. Span 112 ft. 6 in.; length 105 ft.; maximum speed 525 m.p.h.

Patterns

Cut out and shape fuselage. The nose is made separately and glued to the tab projecting from the fuselage. The cockpit window goes round the front of the nose, and the ends of this pattern can be put into the space between the main body and the nose cone.

Make wing and tailplane in two halves; make fin. All from double thickness.

87

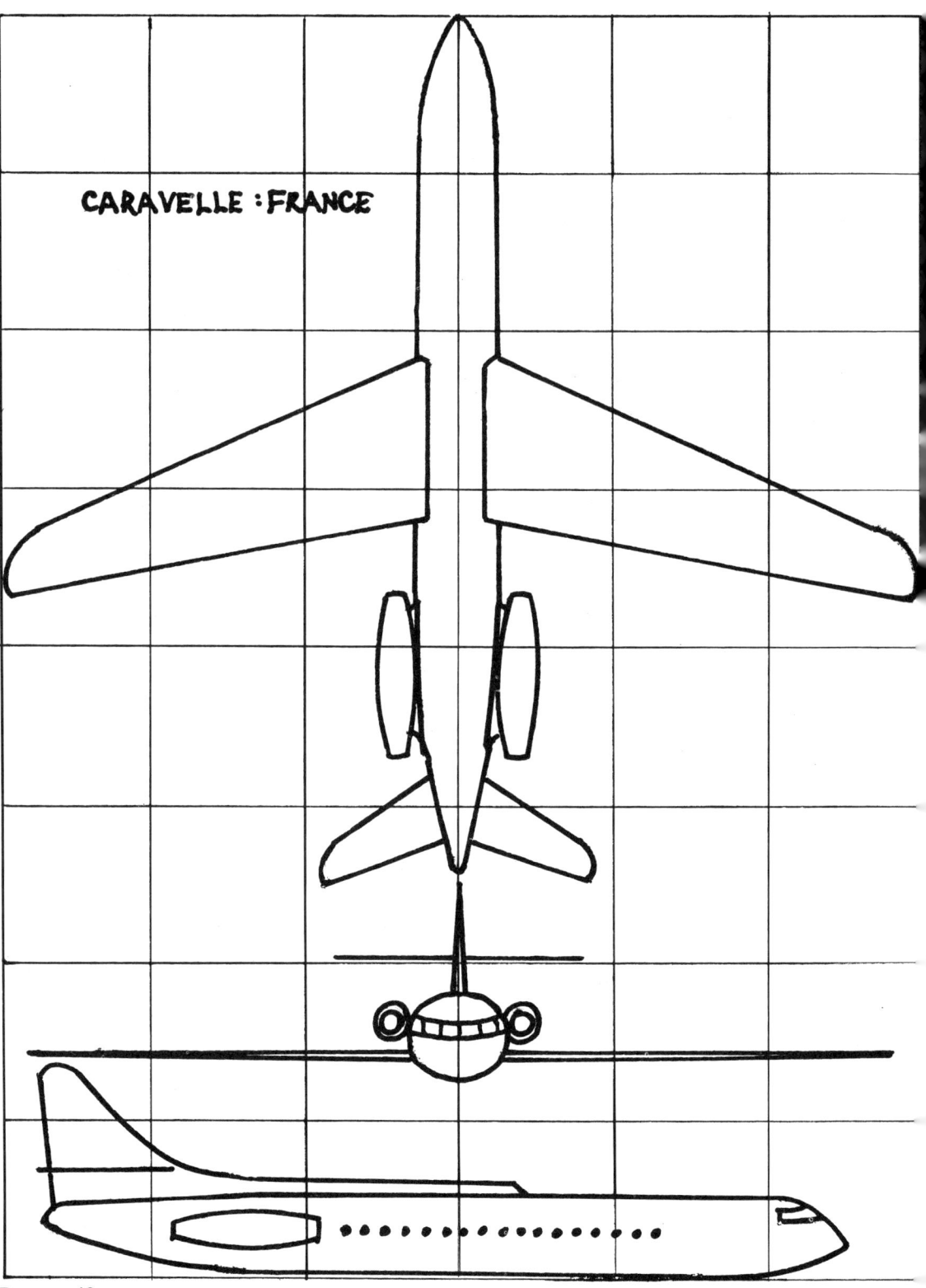

CARAVELLE : FRANCE

PLATE 42

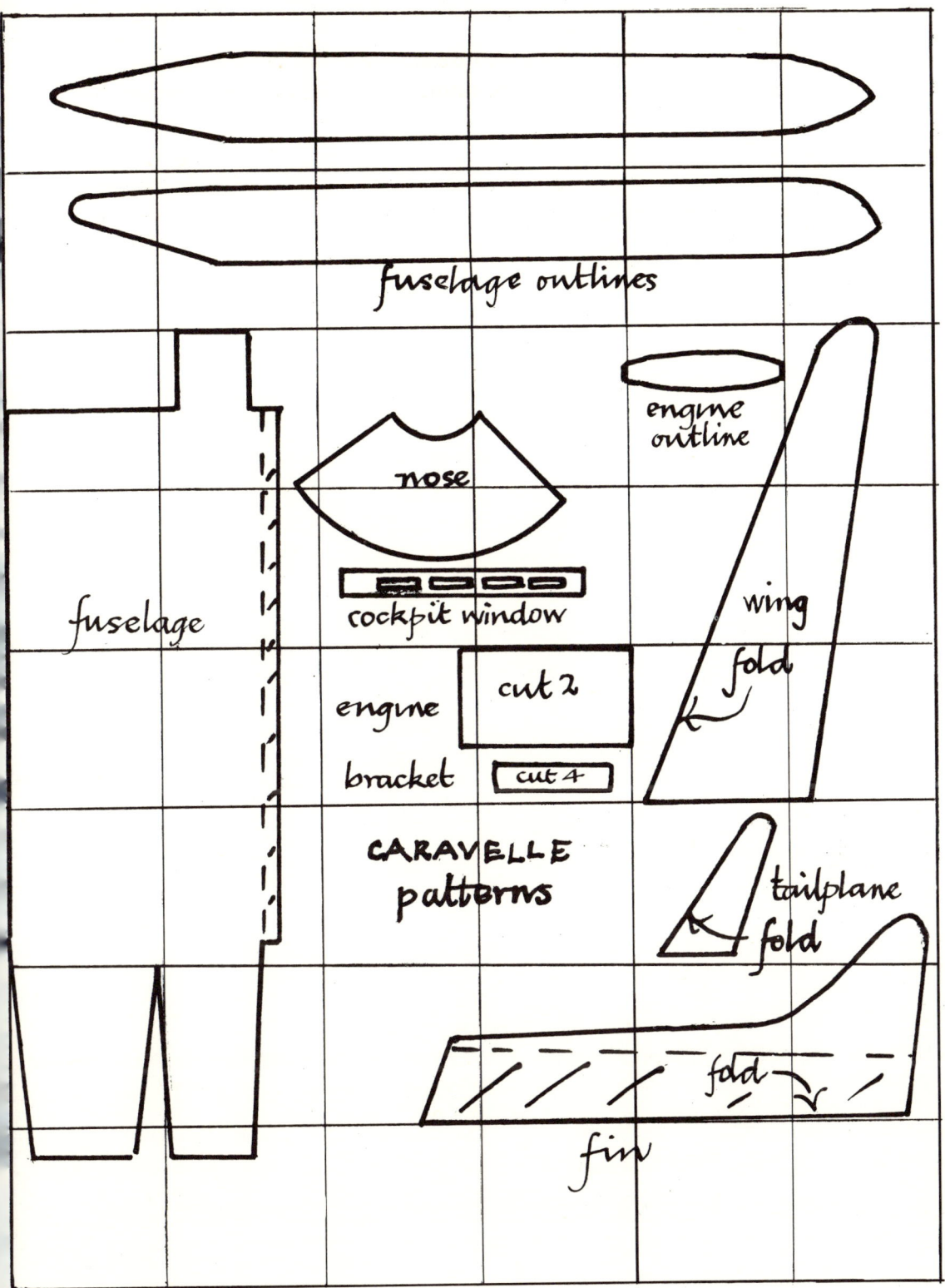

fuselage outlines

nose

engine outline

fuselage

cockpit window

engine bracket

cut 2

cut 4

wing

fold

CARAVELLE patterns

tailplane

fold

fold

fin

PLATE 43

Make a slit along the back of the fuselage to take the fin; note that part of the front of the fin comes above the fuselage. The tailplane is attached to the fin.

Cut slits in fuselage and glue in wing halves: check position on Plate 42.

Make two engines by rolling the patterns into tubes. Attach the engines to the body with small brackets. Make a bracket by gluing two bracket pieces together in the middle and then opening the two pieces to form an H shape.

6 (a) · A Stand for Models

Materials: One piece of balsa wood $3'' \times 3''$ and $\frac{1}{4}''$ thick; two pieces $\frac{1}{2}''$ square balsa strip each $3''$ long, two pieces $\frac{1}{2}''$ square balsa strip $2''$ long. One $2''$ wooden ball. Piece of thin pliable wire. Refer to Plate 1.

1. Draw in diagonals on square piece of wood to find centre. Set compasses to a radius of $\frac{3}{4}''$ and draw circle on wood from centre.
2. Cut out the circle of wood. This can be done with a sharp knife.
3. Glue balsa strip to underside of above piece at edges. On Plate 1 bbb represents this strip: a is the square top.
4. Pierce a hole in the wooden ball and push in the wire.

The ball rests in the hole made by removing the circle of wood. The wire can be bent at the top to make a clip or it can be put into the fuselage of the model. The finished stand can be stained or painted. The position of the model can be altered at will, as the ball remains loose.

(b) · A Papier Mâché Fuselage

Materials: Plasticine, Vaseline, tissue paper, thin paste and glue.

1. Make fuselage shape from plasticine.
2. Grease shape with Vaseline.
3. Cut tissue paper (white) into small squares and stick a layer of these to the plasticine shape with Vaseline. This is to prevent paste sticking to the plasticine.
4. Paste a layer of tissue paper squares over the Vaseline layer.

5. Paste on four more layers of tissue paper squares—five in all should be enough for a small model. When pasting on the squares, see that each square overlaps the preceding one, taking care with each layer to get an even and complete coverage: smooth each layer down well.

6. When the papier mâché is quite dry, draw a pencil line around the centre of the fuselage shape lengthwise; cut round this line with a sharp knife—it may not be necessary to cut the papier mâché entirely in half. Ease open the casing and remove the plasticine.

7. Rejoin the papier mâché case by gluing the cut edges. The join is then sealed and hidden with squares and paste.

8. When dry, the shape can be made smoother if necessary with some fine glasspaper.

7 · Books about Aircraft

The drawings of aeroplanes in this book are true in general outline; they do not show detail. The reason for this is to simplify their construction in paper. If you want to find out more about these and other aircraft, the following books are recommended.

Janes All the World's Aircraft: published annually. A large book usually to be found in local reference libraries. Published by Sampson Law, London.

The Aircraft of the World: 3rd edition 1965. A very good overall survey with profiles and photographs compiled by William Green, who has written several books about aeroplanes. Published by Macdonald and Co., London.

The Pocket Encyclopaedia of World Aircraft in Colour: by Kenneth Munson, published by the Blandford Press, London, from 1966 onwards. A number of handy-sized well-produced books with good colour illustrations.

Profile Publications: A really excellent series of pamphlets on individual aircraft, each written by an expert on the aircraft dealt with, and containing fine illustrations in colour both of the aircraft and its markings. Some of these pamphlets have been bound into volumes, which local reference libraries may possess. Individual pamphlets can also be obtained direct from the publisher: Profile Publications, Coburg House, Sheet Street, Windsor.

Encyclopaedia of World Aircraft: a popular account covering past, present and future, suitable for a boy's bookshelf; by John W. R. Taylor, published by Odhams Books Ltd. in 1966.

Aircraft (Picture Reference Books): published in 1967 by Brockhampton Press. An easily-read, inexpensive booklet containing many drawings and a bird's-eye view of aircraft history.

H.M.S.O. Publications:

The World's First Aeroplane Flights (1903–1908), 1965

A Brief History of Flying from Myth to Space Travel, 1967

Aeronautics: 1. Early Flying, 1966

Aeronautics: 2. Flying since 1913, 1966

All written by C. H. Gibbs-Smith, and obtainable from the Stationery Office.

49 High Holborn, London, W.C.1. These publications can also be bought at the Science Museum, South Kensington, London, where there is a special section devoted to aircraft exhibits containing past and present planes. You can see a fascinating collection of historic aircraft, so arranged that the visitor can get a good look at them.